Schools' Liabilities to Pupils and Parents

Joanna Grainger
Adrian Parkhouse
and
Elizabeth Potter

Croner Publications Ltd
Croner House
London Road
Kingston upon Thames
Surrey KT2 6SR
Telephone: 0181-547 3333

Copyright © 1999 Croner Publications Ltd

Published by
Croner Publications Ltd
Croner House
London Road
Kingston upon Thames
Surrey KT2 6SR
Telephone: 0181-547 3333

While every care has been taken
in the writing and editing of this book,
readers should be aware that only Acts of Parliament
and Statutory Instruments have the force of law,
and that only the Court can authoritatively
interpret the law.

British Library Cataloguing-in-Publication Data.
A catalogue record for this book
is available from the British Library.

ISBN 1 85524 524 8

Printed by Creative Print and Design, Wales

THE AUTHORS

Elizabeth Potter, Adrian Parkhouse and Joanna Grainger are solicitors in the London firm of Farrer & Co and specialise in employment law, litigation and charity law respectively.

Elizabeth qualified as a solicitor in 1979 and worked on employment law issues in the National Coal Board Legal Department for six years, in the period up to and including the miners' strike. She then joined Farrer & Co in 1985, becoming a partner in 1988. Elizabeth is also a Part-Time Employment Tribunal Chairman.

Adrian qualified as a solicitor in 1984, becoming a partner in 1989 specialising in litigation.

Joanna qualified as a solicitor in 1993 and was involved in education law research whilst lecturing at City University. She then returned to private practice to pursue her interest in charity and education law issues, joining Farrers in 1997.

All three are members of Farrer & Co's Education Group which draws expertise from a number of the firm's specialist work-type teams to service the diverse needs of the Education sector. Education Group clients include a wide range of schools, universities, and post-graduate establishments.

The authors regularly lecture and write on Education Law topics.

THE REVIEWER

Anthony Woodard taught for 27 years in maintained secondary schools, becoming head of a comprehensive school in Surrey. He worked at Croner Publications for several years before finishing his full-time career as Deputy Director of Education for the Archdiocese of Southwark.

Anthony continues as external editor of Croner's *The Head's Legal Guide* and is secretary to the Education Law Association. He is a governor of a voluntary-aided school in West Sussex.

CONTENTS

INTRODUCTION

Education law before the 1990s focused predominantly on the esoteric, depersonalised concepts of public law and statutory duties. Now, in a litigious consumer society, the focus is on individual rights and entitlements and there is an expectation of damages for the individual where those rights are not fulfilled. Schools and their governors are finding that education law increasingly revolves around individual challenges, whether by pupils or their parents.

Some of the causes of this cultural change (and perhaps reflections of it) have been key public policy decisions by the House of Lords. For many years, doctors and lawyers (for example) have faced the risk of negligence claims relating to the performance of their professional duties. Education professionals are now in the same position. In the landmark decision of the House of Lords in the cases of *Dorset*, *Hampshire* and *Bromley*, Lord Browne Wilkinson stated:

> In my judgement, a school which accepts a pupil assumes responsibility not only for his physical well-being but also for his educational needs. The education of the pupil is the very purpose for which the child goes to the school.

Much of this book is an explanation of the consequences of this decision.

The challenge to schools is perhaps most novel and acute in the area of educational standards. The world of education has already done a great deal to define, audit and submit to public scrutiny its achievements and weaknesses. Schools now live with the rigours of Ofsted inspections, and academic league tables. The national curriculum and SATS are a fact of life.

The first issue that this book will seek to address is what Governors have to fear in relation to challenges from parents and pupils if children's educational attainment (as measured against current benchmarks), does not match parental or pupil expectations. This area of the law is still undeveloped in the UK (and in other common law jurisdictions, such as the US and Australia), although the number of challenges is mounting. Therefore, there is much fear, much identification of hypothetical risks and threats, without much solid experience as to how far the courts are prepared to go in giving individuals enforceable rights. Our aim will be to form a balanced view as to the possibilities for pupils and their parents of using the law of negligence, breach of contract and breach of statutory duty to challenge the educational performance of schools.

Special Educational Needs

The creation of the Special Educational Needs Tribunal (SENT) in 1994 coincided with the *Dorset, Hampshire* and *Bromley* decision. It gave a new opportunity for parents to challenge — on an individual basis — the adequacy of the provision made for their children with special educational needs. It heightened parental expectations of schools and encouraged recourse to litigation if those expectations were not met. The creation of the SENT was accompanied by new Department for Education and Employment (DfEE) Circulars and a new Code of Practice on the Identification and Assessment of Special Educational Needs. These documents produced new administrative duties for schools. In imposing new duties on schools, the Circulars and code also created clearer evidence of schools not making provision in accordance with best practice.

References and Grade Predictions

Carrying on with the theme of educational rights and entitlements we will consider schools' potential liability in relation to references and grade predictions. This is another field where a landmark ruling of the House of Lords in 1994 made the public policy decision to allow challenges in negligence. What is the potential liability of the individual teacher (and vicariously of the school or local educational authority (LEA) that employs that teacher) for an unfavourable job reference for a pupil leaving school? What is the risk if a teacher makes an A-level grade prediction, a child is not then accepted at a certain university, and the prediction subsequently seems unreasonably pessimistic when the examination results are announced?

Admissions and Exclusions

Admissions and exclusions can be similarly emotive. There has been a 75% increase in admission appeals since 1992 — over a thousand of the 12,500 exclusions in 1996/97 were appealed. The lessons that can be learned from the case law on admissions and exclusions are examined in Chapter 7.

Pupils' Physical Well-being

Schools' liability for the physical well-being of their pupils is perhaps a better understood, more mature topic. The potential of liability for failure to control the under-15s' scrum or for lack of supervision of children participating in outdoor pursuits is well understood but what is current good practice? What is the standard that can be expected of the reasonable school?

Incidents such as the Dunblane shooting have brought into sharper focus the question of schools' duty to protect pupils on school premises, whether from intruders or, indeed, from fellow pupils. What dangers are reasonably foreseeable? What responses to those dangers are reasonably practicable? This is an area where developments in parental expectations tend to be driven by sensation and the challenge is to find a prudent level of response.

Bullying, Physical Harm and Substance Abuse

In Chapters 4, 5 and 6 respectively, we examine the issues of bullying, child abuse and substance abuse. One of the difficulties with these topics is that they attract rather melodramatic coverage in the media. The challenge in such a heated environment is to draw balanced, practical conclusions as to good practice.

Be Positive!

The list of potential risks and claims can seem daunting for Governors but it is important to maintain a sense of perspective. The level of claims against schools and education professionals is still very low, compared to other sectors such as medicine. The challenge for all those in the education sector is to do their part to keep it like this. Individual, often much-reported, cases will highlight the changing expectations that society and the law have of schools. They highlight to Governors areas where there could be a potential exposure. They should not engender fear and panic that vast numbers of claims are inevitable — and that losing those claims is inevitable.

Schools have worked extremely hard to develop clear policies and implement best practice. Governors need to be confident that if they concentrate on monitoring that their schools are being run in accordance with their policies and good practice, the risk of claims will fall and the chances of them winning any claims made will rise. Then the risk of legal claims is put into its true perspective. It should be a check and balance on the perimeter of school life, not a dominant, centre-stage issue.

CHAPTER 1

THE LIABILITY OF A SCHOOL TO PARENTS AND PUPILS

Parents and pupils are increasingly prepared to take legal action over grievances. In the independent sector, parents are more likely to bring an action in contract, alleging that they have not received the service they paid for. In the state sector, where it is much more difficult to show that a contract exists between the school and the parent, it is more likely that the pupil will bring an action in negligence for compensation. Typically, the pupil will argue that the school has failed to diagnose dyslexia, deal adequately with bullying, or give careful predictions of expected grades or careful references, and that this has resulted in emotional or behavioural difficulties for the pupil as well as damaging his or her future prospects. In order to succeed, the pupil must show that a duty of care exists, that it has been breached and that the breach has caused the loss which the pupil complains of and that this damage was foreseeable. However, these hurdles are steep and the courts take a robust view, being reluctant to extend liability.

Even in the independent sector, claims in *negligence* may become more common as the action can be brought by the pupil against the school. The pupil may qualify for legal aid and this may make the option of bringing a case in negligence attractive.

GENERAL LIABILITY FOR NEGLIGENCE

The key case which opened the door to claims by pupils in tort alleging that the school or teacher has been negligent is *X v Bedfordshire County Council*. It is, therefore, worth looking at this case in some detail.

Case Summary

The case of *X and Others (Minors) v Bedfordshire County Council* [1995] 3 All ER 353 is a House of Lords decision in a "consolidated interlocutory appeal". This means that it is an appeal on a point of law and the facts alleged by the parties do not have to be proved but are assumed to be true by the court.

The question for the court to decide was whether, even if the facts alleged were true, the defendants would have any cause of action. Consequently, the judgment does not discuss the very real problems of actually proving that negligence occurred and that it caused the loss which the plaintiff alleged he had suffered. The issue of liability on the facts of *Christmas v Hampshire County Council* [1995] 3 All ER 353, 394 have now been considered and these are discussed below.

The facts

The case is particularly complicated because it deals with five cases together, with different facts. The full title of the case is *X and Others (Minors) v Bedfordshire County Council* in *re M (a minor)*, in *re E (a minor)*, and *Keating v London Borough of Bromley*.

These five appeals can be divided into two groups. The first two cases (abuse cases) are concerned with allegations that public authorities negligently carried out or failed to carry out their statutory duties to protect children from abuse. *X v Bedfordshire County Council* concerned five children who had been living in squalid conditions and it was felt that

2

the county council had failed to take adequate steps to alleviate the situation. *Re M* concerned alleged negligence in the identification of the abuser of a child which led to a child being unnecessarily separated from her mother causing both of them to suffer from anxiety neurosis. There is also an allegation in *re M* that the public authorities were vicariously liable for a breach of duty of care to the plaintiffs committed by the professionals employed by them.

The remaining cases (education cases) concerned a failure by the education authorities to carry out statutory duties imposed on them by the **Education Acts 1944–1981** in relation to children with special educational needs.

In *re E (a minor)*, E alleged that the county council failed to diagnose or make proper provision for his special educational needs. He claimed damages for breach of statutory duty and negligence. The claim in negligence was formulated in a number of alternative ways.

1. That the authority negligently failed to make a proper statement or make proper provision for his special educational needs.

2. That the authority provided a psychology service which negligently advised the plaintiff's parents, who relied on such advice.

3. That the psychologists and the officers employed by the authority owed a personal duty of care to use professional skill and care in their assessment and advice, for breach of which the authority was vicariously liable.

The *Hampshire* case again concerned an allegation that the defendant authority was vicariously liable for the negligence of the Head and the county advisory service. It was claimed that if dyslexia had been correctly diagnosed, appropriate remedial treatment would have been instituted and the plaintiff's educational handicap, together with the subsequent problems in his development which it generated, would have been ameliorated.

The *Bromley* case concerned an allegation that the Borough at certain times failed to provide a place for the plaintiff at any school. The case considered whether an action could be brought for breach of statutory duty and whether an action could be brought in tort alleging negligence. The issues raised are discussed below.

Breach of Statutory Duty

One of the arguments is that the plaintiffs should recover for "breach of statutory duty", in other words for the failure of the relevant authorities to comply with their duties under statute. The House of Lords has made it clear that there can be no private law claim for damages in an action for breach of statutory duty, by confirming that the claim in the abuse cases and the education cases was rightly struck out on this basis.

This is because the statutes in question are construed as protecting the interests of the public as a whole rather than imposing rights upon a defined class of the public. Consequently to grant a remedy for breach of statutory duty went against the general principle of statutory interpretation, which states that the court must look at the intention of Parliament and beware imposing a liability wider than that which the legislature could have contemplated.

One way of discerning the intention of Parliament is to consider whether the statutory duty was imposed for the protection of a limited class of persons and whether the statute provides some other means of enforcing rights. Section 326 of the **Education Act 1996**, for example, provides a right of appeal against the special educational provision specified in a statement of special educational needs. It is, therefore, unlikely that Parliament also intended to confer a right to sue for damages as this right is not explicitly set out. A remedy is provided to parents who are dissatisfied in that they can appeal to the SENT.

It seems to be clear that the way to enforce the performance of statutory duties is by *judicial review*. This may result in a review of the decision but not a remedy of damages. Judicial review is the examination by a court of an administrative decision to determine whether the decision was made properly. The review looks at the decision-making process in an attempt to ensure that the substance of the decision was reached in accordance with the law.

Common Law Duty of Care

The first hurdle that a pupil must overcome in bringing an action in negligence is to demonstrate that he or she is owed a common law duty of care. One of the key issues in this case is whether — despite the fact that the area is covered by statutory duty — there can be a parallel duty of care at common law. One of the difficulties in holding that a duty of care exists, together with a statutory duty, is that very often, a statutory duty confers an element of discretion on the public authority as to the extent to which the duty is to be performed. It is unlikely that a public authority in exercising its discretion, which is by its very nature subjective, will not occasionally disappoint some people. It clearly cannot be right for those who are angered by the fact that discretion was not exercised in their favour to be able to sue for damages.

The ordinary principles of negligence apply, however, if the plaintiff's complaint alleges carelessness not in the taking of a discretionary decision to do some act but in the way that act had been performed. The question whether or not there is a common law duty of care has to be decided by applying the usual principles. These are laid down in *Caparo Industries plc v Dickman* [1990] 1 All ER 568, 573–574, where it was held that it is necessary to show that:

- the damage to the plaintiff was reasonably foreseeable

- the relationship between the plaintiff and the defendant is sufficiently proximate

- it is just and reasonable to impose a duty of care.

Consequently, in *re E (a minor)*, where the claim was that the authority provided a psychology service which negligently advised the plaintiff's parents who relied on such advice, it was held that the LEA, having exercised its discretion in deciding to offer a psychological service to the public, could be held to owe a duty of care to the public not to operate this service in a negligent way.

Vicarious Liability

It is possible that — *in addition to* incurring liability for a breach of a direct duty of care — the relevant authority can also be indirectly or vicariously liable for the breaches of professional duty owed by its employees.

THE IMPLICATIONS OF THE DECISION IN X v BEDFORDSHIRE COUNTY COUNCIL

The case is of fundamental importance because it established that teachers *did* owe a duty of care to pupils when providing education and therefore their employer (either the LEA or the governing body in the case of grant-maintained schools and voluntary aided schools) could therefore be vicariously liable for their actions. Even if the child is able to establish (following *X v Bedfordshire County Council*) that the teacher owed him or her a duty of care, it has to be shown how that duty has been breached and that the breach has actually caused damage. It is important to remember that these cases are only dealing with the possibility of bringing a claim in theory. However, even if a pupil is able to establish that he or she is owed a duty of care, there are further obstacles to overcome.

WHY IS IT DIFFICULT FOR A CHILD TO BRING AN ACTION IN NEGLIGENCE?

Standard of Care

One of the difficulties lies in establishing the standard of care teachers can be held to. Teachers should not be held to a standard that is higher than other professionals and be liable for mere errors of judgment. The case that establishes the standard of care a professional owes is *Bolam v Friern HMC* [1957] 1 WLR 582 586.

> The test is the standard of the ordinary skilled man exercising and professing to have that special skill. A man need not possess the highest expert skill at the risk of being found negligent. It is well-established law that it is sufficient if he exercises the ordinary skill of an ordinary competent man exercising that particular art...there may be one or more perfectly proper standards and if a medical man conforms with one of those proper standards then he is not negligent...a mere personal belief that a particular technique is best is no defence unless that belief is based on reasonable grounds.

The conclusion is that it is only if a teacher embarks on a course of action that no reasonable teacher would pursue that he or she risks liability in negligence. This is made clear in the judgment [1995] All ER 353, 396.

> The head teacher and the advisory teacher were only bound to exercise the skill and care of a reasonable head teacher and advisory teacher. The Bolam test will apply and the judge at the trial will have to decide whether or not the advice tendered by the head teacher and advisory teacher was in accord with the views that might have been entertained at the time by reasonable members of the teaching profession.

Causation

Even if the teacher or LEA has fallen below the standards of a reasonable teacher or LEA, there are still difficulties of causation. It is apparent that the plaintiff will need to adduce evidence to show that the adverse consequences of a congenital defect could have been mitigated by early diagnosis of the defect and appropriate treatment. The plaintiff will also need to adduce evidence that either the diagnosis was careless or the treatment was not provided. The plaintiff must show that it was more likely than not that the tort caused or made a material contribution to the damage.

Type of Loss

In all three education cases, the defendant authority submitted that the damage claimed was not recoverable. In *re E (a minor)*, the damage claimed was the cost of providing alternative fee-paying education for the plaintiff. In the *Hampshire* case, Lord Browne Wilkinson made it clear that the plaintiff's advisers should be able to amend the claim so as to allege that the failure properly to treat the plaintiff's dyslexia caused psychological damage sufficiently serious to constitute an identifiable mental illness. In the *Bromley* case, the damage claimed was the impairment of the plaintiff's personal and intellectual development.

In each case, Lord Browne Wilkinson thought that the striking out application was not the appropriate forum for deciding whether damages could be recovered for this loss and that this would be better determined at trial in the light of the plaintiff's actual mental condition and the effect of receiving an inappropriate education.

One of the difficulties with formulating the claim for damages is that if the claim consists of a claim for damages for school fees paid by the parents because they felt the state education provision was inadequate, the loss is incurred by the parents, not by the plaintiff. The court may decide to treat this in the same way as medical and nursing expenses are treated after a plaintiff has been injured in an accident. It may well be that it is not the plaintiff who actually incurs the expense. Very often, the expense is borne by a relative who leaves work to care for a sick relative. However, the loss is still considered to be that of the plaintiff. Second, the fees were incurred because the parents chose to educate the child outside the state system as they were entitled to do. Most parents who choose to educate their children privately do so because they feel in some way dissatisfied with the state provision in their area, yet none of these parents would consider suing the LEA to recover the fees. It is questionable whether the parents in this case should be treated any differently. (For further details, see also "The rights of individuals who receive a defective education", J Holloway, *Education and the Law*, 6(4), p217.)

Another difficulty is whether the plaintiff is actually suing for the loss of the chance of a successful career. Notwithstanding whether the plaintiff could prove on the balance of probability that the tort had caused this loss, it is unclear whether this is a head of damage in tort. One case in which this had been discussed is *Hotson v East Berkshire Area Health Authority* [1987] AC 50. In this case, a boy fell out of a tree and injured his hip. He was taken to hospital, where, as a result of misdiagnosis, he was not treated for a serious condition. By the time the mistake was discovered it was too late to correct it. The judge found that the misdiagnosis only deprived the plaintiff of a 25% chance of recovery. The House of Lords ducked the issue of whether loss of a chance could be a head of damage by saying that, on the balance of probabilities, the plaintiff was in an inoperable position when he arrived at hospital and that therefore the question of recovery for loss of a chance did not arise. This reasoning is slightly flawed since the plaintiff has certainly lost a chance of recovery if, in some cases, surgery following correct diagnosis is successful.

Policy Considerations

The fourth difficulty in this case is that the courts are reluctant to become involved in judging the quality of education.

LIABILITY FOR CONTRACT GENERALLY

Even if the issue is framed as a claim in contract, the issues are essentially the same. The relationship between the school and the parents is defined by contract.

Many independent schools are careful to ensure that parents sign a contract which sets out in considerable detail the responsibilities both of parents and the school. Typically, such a contract addresses issues that include:

- fees
- events requiring notice in writing
- the removal and expulsion of pupils
- the position on insurance for pupils
- the school's responsibility for pupils on the school premises

– the school's responsibility for progress monitoring.

Schools often explicitly state that they do not undertake to diagnose conditions such as dyslexia. Governors should certainly keep contracts under review. If an independent school does not already have a contract with parents, Governors should consider whether to adopt one. However, in determining whether the school delivered the service it promised the courts are likely to have regard to the standards of a reasonable professional teacher and ask whether these standards were satisfied.

The damages payable will be calculated on the basis that the parents should be restored to the position they would have been in if the contract had been performed properly. It is certainly possible for the damages claimed to exceed the school fees paid. However, it is difficult for the parents to succeed in showing they have suffered a loss much beyond this unless they can argue that the child would have supported them in their old age from high earnings. In practice, a claim for breach of contract is often brought as a counterclaim for non-payment of fees.

The governing body of a maintained school now has to adopt a home-school agreement for the school. A home-school agreement is a statement specifying the school's aims and values, the school's responsibilities, the parental responsibilities and the school's expectations of pupils. The governing body should also issue a parental declaration for the parents to sign in which they accept their parental responsibilities and the school's expectations of its pupils.

However, s.111(6) of the **School Standards and Framework Act 1998** provides that a home-school agreement "shall not be capable of creating any obligation in respect of whose breach any liability arises in contract or in tort". In other words, the home-school agreement is unenforceable.

How to Avoid Liability Generally

It is evident that the best way of avoiding a claim for negligence is to create an environment in which the parents consider that the school is doing its best for a child. However, in the event of a claim being made, a school should be in a better position if they take the following steps.

1. Make sure that the Code of Practice on Special Educational Needs is adhered to. This is discussed in more detail in Chapter 2.

2. Make sure all teachers understand their responsibilities and who they should raise any difficulties with.

3. Make sure all records on pupils are kept up to date and detail the steps taken to remedy any problem that is identified.

4. If the school has a contract with the parents, make sure that it is reviewed regularly.

5. Make sure that when a child is disciplined or expelled, proper procedures are followed. These issues are discussed in more detail in Chapter 7 .

6. Make sure that the school is seen to act in accordance with its stated policies.

CHAPTER 2

FAILURE TO DIAGNOSE SPECIAL EDUCATIONAL NEEDS

INTRODUCTION

Failure to diagnose special needs has become a key focus of disputes between parents and schools in recent years, for two reasons:

– the creation of the Special Education Needs Tribunal (SENT) in 1994 invited parents to challenge litigiously the special education provision being made for their children by LEAs

– failure to diagnose special educational needs was identified by the House of Lords in the *Bromley, Dorset* and *Hampshire* cases as an area where negligence liability could in principle arise. (However, this House of Lords decision has been followed by two highly publicised test cases on liability, one of which failed at first instance and the other of which failed in the Court of Appeal but is expected to go to the House of Lords — see below.)

CASE SUMMARIES

Three case summaries are given below, demonstrating the kind of factual situations which can give rise to claims in this area and the current, developing judicial approach to such claims.

"Dyslexic Boy Wins £5000 for Help he Never Received"

This headline comes from the *Daily Telegraph* (20 November 1992). Tony Starkey's parents became concerned about his slow progress in literacy at primary school. They told the Head that they suspected their son was dyslexic but nothing was done. At the request of the parents, the boy was tested for dyslexia when he transferred to secondary school. The school concluded that although he had literacy weaknesses (his reading age was three years behind his chronological age), he was not dyslexic. The parents relied on the opinion of the school, viewing them as the experts.

Four years later, Tony's class teacher contacted the mother to express concern that Tony would fail his GCSEs because of his reading and writing difficulties. The mother then had him tested by the Dyslexia Institute who found that he was dyslexic. In the four years since the school had tested him, his reading age had advanced by just three months. The head of special needs at this secondary school said the Institute's findings had come as a surprise.

Council officials told the court that it was unnecessary to label a child as dyslexic. He was "one of hundreds" of pupils in North Cambridgeshire with literacy difficulties. Some would continue to have problems no matter what provisions were made for them. Mrs Starkey's request for an assessment for special needs was refused because it was unreasonable. The school was providing an appropriate education.

The Local Government Ombudsman concluded that the Council's procedures for preventing children such as Tony from falling through the net were inadequate. The Council's refusal to assess the boy's needs was unreasonable. The Ombudsman ordered the Authority to pay £5000 to Tony and £250 to his parents for their time and trouble in pursuing the matter. He also awarded the costs (estimated at £850) — for the year's lessons that Tony had at the Dyslexia Institute — against the Council.

At the time, the judgment was welcomed by dyslexia campaigners.

> This is an enormously important judgment because LEAs claim that dyslexia doesn't exist. It will send shock waves through the kingdom.

Notes

1. This case was heard in 1992 before the establishment of the SENT. At that stage, parents had to establish that an LEA's overall procedures were inadequate. Now they have the opportunity to complain about the personal provision being made for their child, without having to prove overall procedural inadequacies.

2. This case was seen by dyslexia action groups as a landmark decision, because of previous debates about whether or not dyslexia was a recognised condition. Understanding of conditions such as dyslexia is constantly developing. New conditions needing a response from schools are constantly appearing and becoming medically recognised. For example, *dyspraxia* is currently being cited as "son of dyslexia", the next under-diagnosed and under-treated condition, as dyslexia was10 years ago.

Christmas v Hampshire County Council

Judgment in the case of *Christmas v Hampshire County Council* was given on 24 September 1997 and is useful to demonstrate the successful defence of a school.

1978–1985

While Mark Christmas was at primary school, his mother complained to the Head about her son's progress. Initially, the Head suggested that Mark had a problem with concentration and would do better if he "knuckled down". Subsequently, he was referred by the Head to the LEA's teacher advisory service for examination. The examination was carried out by a teacher adviser who subsequently reported back to the school with a number of recommendations.

Mark's mother remained dissatisfied. He was moved from his village primary school to an independent school specialising in the teaching of children with learning difficulties. He was seen by an educational psychologist at the independent school but dyslexia was not diagnosed and the school gave him no special help. Eventually, his behaviour became so bad that the school recommended he should become a boarder. As the mother had difficulty paying the fees, she (for the first time) approached the LEA, which resulted in the issuing of a statement (a formal statutory statement of a child's special education needs made by the LEA after an assessment of advice from family and relevant professionals) allowing Mark Christmas to continue at the school on a residential basis.

After leaving secondary school, Mark Christmas became a care assistant in a nursing home and then a residential childcare officer at a special school, but found he was denied further promotion because of his learning difficulties. He sued Hampshire County Council, the LEA, claiming damages for injury, loss and damage as a result of LEA employees' failure to identify and diagnose his dyslexia.

The judge's findings

The judge found that after he started at primary school, Mark had been given regular reading tests, only one of which identified a serious gap between his chronological and reading ages. Although Mark sought to rely strongly on this one test, the judge cautioned against taking the results of only one test as definitive. He recognised the possibility of an accidental error in the test or the test being taken on a bad day, and accepted that pupils could vary in performance from term to term and from year to year.

The judge was seriously concerned about the absence of key witnesses in the case because of death or ill health. He was wary of finding negligence against those who were not present to answer for their actions. "Unless there is evidence to point towards some failure on their part I cannot think it is right to assume that they are at fault", he said.

The judge noted that the new school, which was supposed to specialise in teaching children with learning difficulties, did not adopt a different teaching approach from Mark's primary school, for at least two years after Mark arrived there. Nor did it radically differ in its assessment of Mark's main difficulty, which was a failure to concentrate on his work. The judge noted the evidence of Mark Christmas's expert that, while not every child with these difficulties who received help at the primary stage would overcome these difficulties, skilled help from the age he attended the specialist independent school could achieve satisfactory exam results. It followed that if the LEA staff had failed the plaintiff, so too had the staff at the independent school.

The judge concluded that whilst it was perfectly possible for a series of teachers and schools to miss what were well-known difficulties, the improbability of that explanation increased with each opportunity for review. The judge's cautionary conclusion was that not every educational problem could be solved, even if statistically the great majority could be evaluated or overcome.

Overall, the judge's conclusion was that the primary school Head, who had experience of special needs and the statement process, had not misread the evidence about Mark Christmas's needs in a way which was inconsistent with the "properly responsible approach to be expected of a competent primary school Head". The judge also concluded that there had not been a failure by the advisory teacher involved in the case. Indeed, he had been "thoughtful and able and free of any criticism". Therefore, he concluded that there had not been a breach of the duty of care by the Council and dismissed the case.

Phelps v The Mayor and Burgesses of the London Borough of Hillingdon

This case dealt with the unresolved issues on duty of care in a judgment given on 10 October 1997 in the High Court, and on 4 November 1998 in the Court of Appeal.

Pamela Phelps was born in 1973. When attending infant school, Pamela was referred to the LEA's psychologist for "lack of education progress". The educational psychologist who was initially consulted confirmed that the girl was under-functioning and suggested time, patience and interest were her major problems. She referred Pamela to a Child Guidance Clinic, where she was seen by a psychiatric social worker and a psychotherapist. The director of the clinic also saw her and concluded that her home circumstances were principally to blame for her difficulties. Pamela's parents and her junior school continued to have concern because she did not improve.

Pamela's problems appeared to increase after she moved to secondary school in 1985 and she was referred to another educational psychologist who produced a short report which, although expressed to be confidential, was discussed with Pamela's parents. Although a reading test and other assessments were carried out, the psychologist did not include the recorded figures in her report. Instead, she simply used verbal descriptions. She concluded that Pamela was seriously under-performing in reading and spelling but suggested that in order to make progress, she should concentrate on developing her confidence. The report made no reference to special difficulties or dyslexia.

From 1985 until she left school in 1990, little was done for Pamela by the educational psychologist or the school, despite her parents' increasing desperation at her lack of progress.

February 1990

Pamela was finally diagnosed as having special learning difficulties in February 1990. By then, however, the LEA seemed to have considered it too late to do anything further for her. After leaving school, Pamela received some tuition from the Dyslexia Institute but her employment was limited to assembly line work or routine processing or packing.

Pamela sued her LEA, the London Borough of Hillingdon, claiming she should have been diagnosed as dyslexic in 1985. She also claimed that her continuing under-performance required further inquiries and investigation and that if she had been taught in a manner appropriate to her needs, her standard of literacy would have been enhanced and her frustrations and anxieties avoided.

The LEA's defence was that the role of the educational psychologist was to advise the LEA and the school, not the parents. Also the educational psychologist was only part of a multi-disciplinary team involved in Pamela's welfare and her report was only one factor to be taken into account in determining her educational needs. The same argument was used in defence of the school. So, in the High Court, the LEA concentrated on trying to prove that no duty was owed, rather than on proving that the individuals involved had not been in breach of their particular duties of care.

The High Court judge found that educational psychologists owe a duty of care to children they examine because they know their findings, recommendations and advice will be acted upon by the child through his or her parents. In addition, in this case, the parents were genuinely concerned about the child's lack of progress and wanted to do the best for her. They could, therefore, be relied upon to have implemented the educational psychologist's advice. The judge also found that the educational psychologist had a duty of care to the LEA and the schools.

The judge concluded that there had been a breach of the duty of care by the educational psychologist in failing to diagnose Pamela's special learning difficulties. They should have been spotted. The concentration on her behaviour and home environment was misjudged.

> This was more than an error of judgement; it was a failure to exercise a degree of care and skill to be expected of an ordinarily competent member of her profession. She was, of course, newly qualified and of limited experience...there is a permissible inference that she may have been

reluctant to disagree with her [senior officers] by carrying out further tests or instigating further enquiries to determine whether or not emotional problems alone could explain the plaintiff's special learning difficulties. Nonetheless, in my view the evidence is overwhelming that she could and should have looked further but did not.

The judge also found that the educational psychologist should have reconsidered her conclusions and recommendations when she saw that Pamela had made so little progress, despite the specialist teaching provided by the school and in the light of the child's parents' continuing anxiety.

As regards the school, the judge was satisfied that the school could owe a duty of care to an under-performing pupil but on the evidence, the teachers had neither ignored the matter nor failed to make any attempt to deal with it. They were entitled to rely on the advice of the educational psychologist. Although she may have been wrong, in the circumstances, the fact that the school failed to teach Pamela specifically as a dyslexic did not place it in breach of its duty of care. It was not negligent in failing to challenge the educational psychologist's conclusions. The judge found the LEA vicariously liable for the breaches of duty of the educational psychologist.

Considering damages, the judge rejected the LEA's argument that Pamela had not suffered any recognised personal injury. He found that the injury included "a failure to mitigate the adverse consequences of congenital defect". He concluded that, even though the responses of dyslexics to support were variable, "the adverse consequences of the plaintiff's dyslexia could have been mitigated by the early diagnosis and appropriate treatment or educational provision" and that she was entitled to damages. These were assessed at £7000 for past and future tuition and equipment, £25,000 for future loss of earnings and £12,500 for general damages.

The Court of Appeal's decision

The Court of Appeal reversed the decision of the High Court, concluding that an educational psychologist employed by an LEA, to whom a child had been referred for assessment, did not owe a duty of care to the child unless it was clear that, in addition to performing her duty to her employers, she assumed personal responsibility to the child.

Dyslexia was a congenital condition and not an injury. Failure to ameliorate its effects was not an injury. Damages could only be awarded if the injury was exacerbated by delayed treatment, or there was greater or more prolonged pain and suffering.

However, the fact that dyslexia was not an injury was not conclusive of the fact that damages were irrecoverable. Damages for economic loss were recoverable in such circumstances if there had been an assumption of responsibility to protect the plaintiff from the type of loss sustained.

An educational psychologist who was consulted privately by parents concerned at the lack of literacy progress of their child, could be liable in contract for failing to take reasonable care in diagnosing dyslexia, if it was in the reasonable contemplation of the parties that the child would as a result be seriously handicapped in achieving literacy. However, in this case, the Court of Appeal concluded that the educational psychologist had not assumed or undertaken personal responsibility towards the child to take reasonable care to assess her educational potential and provide strategies to improve her position.

In reaching this decision, the Court of Appeal expressed concern about the effects of the *Dorset, Hampshire* and *Bromley* cases. The fact that the House of Lords had concluded that an individual educational psychologist or teacher might be liable had led to a proliferation of claims. The risk was that the immunity of LEAs to claims, granted for powerful policy reasons, would be completely circumvented.

It would be a matter for very great concern if the policy considerations which led the House of Lords to hold that such actions would not lie against the LEA direct, could be so easily circumvented by reference to the alleged liability of its employees. It was undesirable that LEAs should find themselves, as in the present case, contesting a case many years after the event, when many of the relevant documents were no longer available and witnesses could not be traced.

Where now on liability for dyslexia?

The lingering uncertainty in this case is that leave has been granted for an appeal to the House of Lords. The pattern in the *Dorset, Hampshire* and *Bromley* cases, mirrored in *Spring v Guardian Assurance* (see Chapter 3), was that the Court of Appeal held out against extension of liability for negligence on public policy grounds and had their decisions overturned by the House of Lords.

Will the House of Lords do the same in this case? A clear position on the likelihood of success in claims for failure to diagnose and meet special needs has not yet been reached.

PRINCIPLES ARISING FROM THESE CASES

The Head and teachers clearly owe a duty to exercise the skill and care of a reasonable Head or teacher in assuming responsibility for a child's educational needs, ie:

– taking reasonable steps to address known under-performance

– taking reasonable care when providing education advice to parents.

Educational psychologists and similar professionals owe a duty to use reasonable professional skill and care in the assessment of a child's special educational needs. However, it is not yet finally resolved precisely in what circumstances educational psychologists or other advisers, asked to assess a child by the LEA, can be sued. The likelihood is that parents and children will have to show clear evidence that the psychologist assumed personal responsibility to them, as well as to the LEA.

The standard expected of education professionals is going to be whether they acted outside the standards of reasonable members of their profession at the time. There will be lower expectations of teachers dealing with a classroom of children and who have less specialist training in conducting individual assessments of special needs than of specialist advisors.

Damages will be awarded if there is proof that the relevant education professionals assumed responsibility for protecting a child from the form of loss that was subsequently sustained. However, a condition such as dyslexia should not simply be viewed as injury. Damages will only be awarded where the condition was exacerbated by delayed treatment or pain and suffering was exacerbated by the delay.

Independent schools are open to challenge, whether in negligence or contract, for failure to diagnose and deal with learning difficulties, although actions to date have been focused on LEAs.

WHAT ARE THE LIKELY FUTURE DEVELOPMENTS?

Will More be Expected of Schools?

All these reported cases relate to events before the SENT structure and supporting Code of Practice were put in place. Such delay in litigation of this nature will be common because individual pupils will tend not to start legal actions until they have finished education and failed to obtain their desired career progress. However, this delay means that the outcome of reported cases must be treated with caution — it will not be a reliable guide to what is expected of schools currently. For example, attitudes and practice in relation to dyslexia have developed very significantly since the early 1980s. Schools will now be measured against late 1990s best practice.

Greater Responsibility on Parents?

To discourage burgeoning litigation, LEAs may in future seek to place greater responsibility on parents for a child's education. Parents have the overriding duty to secure a child's education. The LEA could seek to blame the parents when they remove the child from school or fail to support the child with any remedial work. The first step would be to blame the parents, to avoid liability. The second step would be to join the parents as defendants. Are parents open to action for failing to implement advice from the school or for failing to request an assessment of their child's educational needs? What part do home-school agreements have in this debate in future?

Special Needs Cases as Personal Injury Cases

In personal injury cases, special procedural rules permit discovery of relevant documents before legal proceedings are issued. The English courts are currently deciding whether special needs cases fall within the personal injury definition. In *Anderton v Clwyd County Council* 4 February [1998], the judge in the High Court upheld an order for pre-proceedings discovery in a case where a young woman was claiming that there had been a failure to diagnose her dyslexia at primary school, with the result that her educational and personal skills were underdeveloped, and that she suffered loss of self-esteem and long-term psychological problems. The judge relied on a statement by the judge in the *Phelps* case in the High Court in reaching his conclusion. "I am prepared to regard injury as including a failure to mitigate the adverse consequences of a congenital defect." However, as in *Phelps*, the Court of Appeal took a different attitude, holding that dyslexia was not akin to a personal injury (*Anderton v Clwyd County Council* [1999] ELR). *Anderton*, too, now appears to be going to the House of Lords so this issue remains unresolved.

BEST PRACTICE DEFINED

It is beyond the scope of this book to provide great detail regarding the SENT (there are several specialist publications available on that subject). The SENT's purpose is to balance pupil and parental desires and concerns against LEA decisions on need and allocation of resources.

What this book *does* consider is the relevance of the SENT and the procedural developments that have accompanied it, to the definition of best practice in this field — and consequently to the definition of practice that falls below best practice and leaves a school (and vicariously the LEA) liable in negligence.

The main DfEE Circulars and the Code of Practice, and the duties they impose on schools — particularly on Governors — are discussed below.

Circular 6/94 — The Organisation of Special Educational Provision

Governors' Responsibilities

The 1996 Education Act puts responsibilities on the governing bodies of maintained schools for making special educational provision for all their pupils with special educational needs. Those responsibilities extend to pupils who do not require statements of special educational needs as well as to the minority with statements. The broad notion is that 20% of children will have special educational needs at some stage in their school career although only about 2% will be statemented. The Circular explains that the Act puts responsibility on the governing bodies of maintained mainstream schools to:

- do their best to secure that necessary provision is made for any pupil who has special educational needs

- secure that, where the responsible person (the Head or the appropriate Governor) has been informed by the LEA that a pupil has special educational needs, those needs are made known to all who are likely to teach the pupil

- secure that teachers in the school are aware of the importance of identifying and providing for those pupils who have special educational needs

- consult the LEA or the governing bodies of other schools where it seems to them necessary or desirable to co-ordinate special educational provision in the area as a whole

- ensure that pupils with special educational needs join in the activities of the school together with pupils who do not have special educational needs, so far as that is reasonably practical and compatible with each pupil receiving the necessary special educational provision, the efficient education of other children in the school and the efficient use of resources

- report annually to parents on their policy for pupils with special educational needs.

Division of responsibilities

The Circular identifies the division of responsibilities for special needs as follows.

1. The *governing body* may choose to appoint a committee to take a particular interest in the school's work on behalf of children with special educational needs.

2. The *Head* is responsible for day-to-day management of all aspects of a school's work, including special educational provision.

3. The *SEN co-ordinator* or team has responsibility for the day-to-day operation of the school's SEN policy.

4. *All teaching and non-teaching staff* should be involved in the development of the school's SEN policy, be fully aware of the school's SEN procedures and be clear about their responsibilities in the implementation of the policy.

5. The *LEA* has responsibility for:

    (a) the identification and the statutory assessment of pupils who require statements of special educational needs

    (b) making statements, arranging provisions set out in statements, and the annual review of those statements (LEAs must also publish details of their SEN policies).

6. *Ofsted*, in inspecting schools, is charged with monitoring schools' provision for pupils with special educational needs, commenting on

the implementation of special needs policies and the extent to which they have had regard to the code of practice.

7. *School policies* need to be formulated and maintained, not only in the light of regulations but having regard to the *Code of Practice on the Identification and Assessment of Special Educational Needs*, the efficient use of resources, the policies of neighbouring mainstream and special schools and the LEA's special needs policy.

Circular 9/94 — The Education of Children with Emotional and Behavioural Difficulties

The duty of the governing body
The duty of the governing body is to ensure that:

- any necessary special education provision is made in their school
- any special educational needs that pupils have are made known to teachers
- teachers are aware of the importance of identifying and providing for pupils with special educational needs as necessary.

The duty of the Head
The Head has a general day-to-day responsibility to ensure that teachers:

- plan lessons
- create an effective learning environment
- have the requisite classroom management skills
- set appropriate work which is differentiated according to ability and aptitude.

Early identification responsibilities of a school
The Circular expects the school and the SEN co-ordinator to have clear and fast-acting communication systems to:

- take appropriate action at the first sign of a pattern of difficulties

- record detailed observations

- explore the nature of the difficulty with the help of the child, the parents, other teachers or the education welfare services and where relevant, the medical and social services

- address the behaviour itself

- structure the child's work to ensure progress

- keep the child as close as possible to the curriculum which his or her peers are receiving so as not to disadvantage the child further

- supplement the school's own expertise where necessary by drawing on advice from outside

- keep detailed records throughout and keep the effectiveness of its approach under regular review.

Partnership with parents

According to the Circular, establishing a partnership with parents is an early priority. Otherwise, parents may feel they are being blamed for the child's difficulties and may avoid contact with the school.

The Code of Practice on the Identification and Assessment of Special Educational Needs

Planning, action and review

The Code puts emphasis on a continuous and systematic cycle of planning, action and review within the school. Responsibility at stage 1 is put on the class teacher or year/form tutor, supported where necessary by the SEN co-ordinator. This stage essentially concerns the gathering of information and registering a child's special educational needs.

At stage 2, observation and exploration of possible solutions need to be progressively refined.

At all times during stages 1 and 2, ie school-based assessment, the school needs to ask itself whether it needs to supplement its own skills and expertise with those of support agencies from outside the school.

Stage 3 involves supplementing school skills with those of support services outside the school, eg learning or behavioural support services, peripatetic teachers, the educational psychology or welfare services, occupational therapists, child health, mental health or social services.

Stages 4 and 5 are shared between the school and the LEA. Stage 4 involves a statutory multidisciplinary assessment of need by the LEA. Stage 5 is that of consideration of the need for a statement by the LEA, recognising that the child's particular needs cannot reasonably be expected to be met from within the resources of the school. If a statement is made, the stage includes monitoring and review of that statement.

Records

The Code puts a high onus on schools to observe and record children's behaviour objectively, the antecedents, the behaviour and the consequences. Records should include:

− school observations

− details of parents' views and their involvement

− the child's views and the involvement of health and social services and other agencies.

The records need to include observations of the child, individual education plans and a record of decisions taken at review meetings.

At stage 3, the SEN co-ordinator or head of the learning support department should ensure that the record is being taken in greater detail, to demonstrate patterns that span time. Dated copies of reports, notes of discussions and minutes of planning meetings, case conferences or interviews with parents should be kept together on the file.

The Governors' practical role

The DfEE Circulars summarised above emphasise the statutory responsibilities on Governors in relation to special educational needs provision within schools. Governors have a formal monitoring role to perform, in relation to implementation of the school's SEN policy. They have a statutory duty to report in each school annual report on implementation of the SEN policy. However, Governors should not be so overwhelmed by the extent of their formal duties that they fail to apply practical common sense to this area of their work. Negligence claims will be successfully resisted not only by having proper formal systems in place but also by ensuring that they are working smoothly in every case, on a personal level. A seriously disaffected parent or pupil is the most likely future litigant. Cases inevitably arise with a difficult personal dimension, that lead to teachers failing to deal with them as expeditiously or effectively as they should. The Governors have a valuable role in such circumstances. They can encourage compliance that has grown slack when difficult cases are not being faced up to by teaching staff.

So the Governors in each school need to consider their role in the special educational needs field, regularly and critically, considering the strengths and weaknesses of special educational needs provision in their school, and the skills and experience they can bring to bear from their own lives. For example, Governors often have valuable professional expertise to offer in relation to record-keeping disciplines. Governors with commercial or professional experience may be able to offer useful practical guidance to teachers, who may not be accustomed to keeping detailed records.

CONCLUSION

Court cases and the SENT have stimulated considerable expectation and willingness to challenge in this field. It is, therefore, an area in which Governors need to be particularly zealous to ensure that best practice is being followed and being documented, so that the school is in the best possible position to defend claims that may be brought many years in the future.

An effective, active sub-committee of Governors that can work with and support the Head and the SEN co-ordinator in this aspect of their work is important in practical terms. Large, formal, Governors' meetings are unlikely to be an appropriate forum for ensuring special needs systems are operating effectively on an individual level. Over time, teachers will grow to trust and appreciate a supportive committee, to which they can bring difficult cases for a more objective view.

CHAPTER 3

LIABILITY FOR CARELESS PREDICTIONS OF GRADES AND CARELESS REFERENCES

INTRODUCTION

Until 1994, the legal position appeared to be that people could only sue in *defamation* in relation to a reference. They could not sue in contract or in tort. The House of Lords decision in *Spring v Guardian Assurance plc* [1994] 3 All ER 129 reversed this position. The *Spring* case related to an employer's duty in giving references about ex-employees to a prospective employer. The extent to which the principles identified in the case apply to a school's duty in giving references for pupils is discussed below.

The Position before the *Spring* Case

The Court of Appeal in the *Spring* case succinctly summarised the old attitude.

> The giver of a reference owes no duty of care in the tort of negligence to the subject of the reference. His duty to the subject is governed by and lies in the tort of defamation. If it were otherwise, the defence of qualified privilege in an action for defamation where a reference was given or the

necessity for the plaintiff to prove malice in an action for malicious false-hood would be by-passed. In effect a substantial section of the law regarding these two associated torts would be emasculated.

The quotation above emphasises the public policy considerations underlying the old view that people could only sue in defamation in relation to references.

Qualified privilege

Lord Diplock described the policy considerations behind the concept of qualified privilege in *Horrocks v Lowe* [1975] AC 133.

> ... as a general rule, English law gives effect to the ninth commandment that a man shall not speak evil falsely of his neighbour. The public interest that the law should provide an effective means whereby a man can vindicate his reputation against calumny has nevertheless to be accommodated to the competing public interest in permitting men to communicate frankly and freely with one another about matters in respect of which the law recognises that they have a duty to perform or an interest to protect in doing so. What is published in good faith on matters of these kinds is published on a privileged occasion. It is not actionable even though it be defamatory and turns out to be untrue. The privilege is not absolute but qualified. It is lost if the occasion which gives rise to it is misused. For in all cases of qualified privilege there is some special reason of public policy why the law accords immunity from suit — the existence of some public or private duty, whether legal or moral, on the part of the maker of the defamatory statement which justifies his communicating it or of some interest of his own which he is entitled to protect by doing so. If he uses the occasion for some other reason he loses the protection of the privilege.

Malice

According to the law of defamation, the defence of "qualified privilege" can be defeated by showing that the person giving the reference was activated by:

– *malice* (ie that the person giving the reference does not believe in the truth of what he or she said

– *some improper motive* (even though he or she believes the truth of what he or she said).

For example, a teacher required to give A-level predictions for university admission applications is giving these predictions "on a privileged occasion". If a teacher intentionally gave unreasonably low predictions not based on performance, for an improper reason, to prevent the pupil obtaining a university place, that could be qualified privilege defeated by malice.

It is very difficult to defeat qualified privilege in complaints about a reference by proving malice, and legal aid is not available for defamation actions. Under the old law, therefore, actions in relation to false or careless references were very rare.

The *Spring* Decision

Duty of care

The House of Lords decision in the *Spring* case was revolutionary because it found that the law of negligence applied to the giving of references.

> An employer who provides a reference concerning an employee or former employee to a prospective employer owes a duty of care to the employee regarding the preparation of the reference and may be liable to him in damages for any economic loss suffered as a result of a negligent misstatement.

Foreseeable loss

According to the *Spring* decision:

> The duty of the employer is to take reasonable care in compiling or giving a reference and in verifying the information on which it is based. Where an employer gives an inaccurate reference about an employee to a prospective employer, it is clearly foreseeable that the employee may be caused financial loss as a result of failing to obtain new employment...In the circumstances, including the importance attached to references in the employment market, it is fair, just and reasonable that the employer should be under an obligation to compensate the employee for any loss caused by the employer's failure to make proper inquiries.

Public policy desirability of strengthening protections against careless references

Where the House of Lords differed most significantly from the attitude of the Court of Appeal (see page 33) was in seeing it as desirable (as a matter of public policy) to strengthen the remedies offered by the law in this field.

> Notwithstanding the existence of the torts of defamation and injurious falsehood, the tort of negligence should be extended to protect the subject where the giver of a reference has said or written what is untrue or where he has acted unreasonably and carelessly in what he has said. The subject of an inaccurate reference is not already adequately protected by the law of defamation. The need there to establish malice in order to defeat the defence of qualified privilege places a wholly disproportionate burden on the employee, since malice is very difficult to prove. Without an action for negligence, an employee may be left with no practical prospect of redress even though the reference may have permanently prevented him from obtaining employment in his chosen vocation. Accordingly, justice requires that the additional cause of action should be available.

Some of the passing comments of the Law Lords on what they believed they were doing to the law of references are also of interest and are listed below.

1.   "There can be no action for negligence if the statement is true."

2.   "Even if it is right that the number of references given will be reduced, the quality and value will be greater and it is by no means certain that to have more references is more in the public interest than to have more careful references. Employers have not been asked to warrant absolutely the accuracy of the facts or the incontrovertible validity of the opinions expressed."

BREACH OF CONTRACT

The House of Lords, in addition to finding that a duty of care arose in negligence, held that a duty of care "may in certain circumstances arise from an implied term of the contract of employment". They considered that there are circumstances in which it is necessary to imply a term into the contract of employment that:

- the employer will provide the employee with a reference at the request of a prospective employer
- the reference will be based on facts revealed after making those reasonably careful enquiries which, in the circumstances, a reasonable employer would make.

The circumstances in which a term might be implied were defined as follows:

- there is a contract of employment or services
- the contract relates to an engagement of a class, where it is normal practice to require a reference from a previous employer before employment is offered
- the employee cannot be expected to enter that class of employment except on the basis that his or her employer will provide a full and frank reference on the employee (when requested by another employer) not later than a reasonable time after termination of a former employment.

This argument is of most relevance in the independent sector, where the relationship between parents and the school is based on contract, although it has less relevance in the state sector.

DISCLAIMERS

One of the Law Lords in *Spring* suggested that the effects of their decision could be mitigated by the use of disclaimers of liability by the giver of the reference. This comment has provoked much speculation — and change of practice — in the commercial world. Disclaimers in references are now common, with typical wording as follows.

This reference is given in good faith but without any legal liability on the part of the company or the author of this reference. It is written and accepted on this basis.

The legal effect of such disclaimers is less certain. The courts would find it unattractive if an employer under a duty of care failed to take care in producing a reference and made untrue or unfounded statements and then sought to hide behind a disclaimer of liability for anything expressed in that reference. They would try and find the employer liable, whatever the disclaimer said. The use of disclaimers is worth due consideration — not as an *alternative* to the use of due care in the preparation of references but as an additional protection.

THE RISK FOR SCHOOLS

As identified in earlier chapters, the *Dorset*, *Hampshire* and *Bromley* cases have clearly brought the law of negligence and the duty of care into the teacher-pupil relationship. The *Spring* case laid down in turn that the law of defamation was not adequate to deal with the issue of references and that the law of negligence should be available for this purpose.

Putting together these two developments, it seems an unavoidable conclusion that liability in negligence can arise in relation to the giving of references and predictions by schools. For pupils aspiring to university admission, the school's A-level predictions are fundamental to their chances of obtaining a desired university place. For non-university candidates, references can be similarly critical to the first job the school leaver obtains. Claims are also conceivable at other stages in the education process, eg incorrect reporting of marks on GCSE or A-level course work or errors by primary schools in reporting SATS results at 11 to receiving senior schools. School reports may be a potential target in due course also, misleading parents about a child's progress, attainment or problems. However, the chances of establishing loss in the earlier stages of schooling will be reduced because it will be more difficult to establish a direct link between a particular error and actual educational outcomes and their economic consequences.

SCHOOL CASES IN THE UK

There have recently been the first signs of legal actions in relation to A-level predictions.

It was widely reported in the press in 1997 that the daughter of Coronation Street's star Mike Baldwin, Johnny Briggs, was bringing an action based on the gap between her predicted grades, a mix of As and Bs in three subjects, and her actual results — D, E and U.

Conversely it was also reported that year that a Vicky Hornby was bringing an action against her school because her A-level predictions were not optimistic enough. She was predicted Bs in English and History and a C in French and on that basis was ruled out from getting a place at a "decent university to read law". She in fact obtained an A and two Bs and sued on the basis that the predictions had prevented her following her long-standing ambition to study law.

It could be contended that such cases clearly demonstrate the argument for reform of the university admissions system. The broad estimate is that half of teachers' A-level predictions are too high — and a quarter too low. Award of places on the basis of actual results, rather than predictions would surely be fairer, if the logistical challenges could be overcome between A-level result announcement date and university start date. It would also relieve teachers of the very difficult, and legally challengeable, task of trying to predict A-level performance nearly a year in advance of the A-level examinations.

PRECAUTIONS AGAINST CLAIMS

In general, schools should seek to operate reference and prediction practices as stringent as those operated by commercial concerns.

Good Record Keeping

The first practical, critical point is good record keeping. Staffing continuity or individual memory should not be relied on. Records of individual attainments, in a form that others can readily interpret, are vital.

Objective Data

Objective data, such as exam results, are the best foundations for safe references. Subjective assessments of pupils based on impressions and hearsay may give useful insights but should be used cautiously. Employers are generally increasingly reticent in the post *Spring* era about expressing critical opinions about employees. If in doubt they merely recite facts, for example length of service and sickness record. This should perhaps send a warning note for teachers. For example, if a new teacher is giving a reference about a pupil they do not know well (and does not necessarily know well, or at all, the previous teacher who has made a subjective critical assessment of the pupil), it would be inadvisable to rely on the previous teacher's views, however strident.

Investigation

The courts consider investigation to be important. It may be tempting to write a reference quickly, under time pressure, knowing that the information on the file is sparse, contradictory or odd and not to cross-check facts or ask the opinion of someone who might be able to fill in important details.

Choice of Words

It is important to give careful thought to each word that is included in (and excluded from) references. It is often useful to write a draft version first.

Cross-checking and Peer Review

Each teacher will bring to the prediction and reference process their own expectations, prejudices and preconceptions. This can easily lead to inequities in references or predictions, within a school or between schools. Governors should consider whether any preconceptions or prejudices are brought to their school's process.

The point is demonstrated by a formal investigation conducted by the Commission for Racial Equality into the admissions processes of St. George's Hospital Medical School. The investigation found that St. George's was a liberal, forward-looking university institution, whose ethos proscribed any form of discrimination. However, because of the discriminatory weightings fed into the computer programme being used for shortlisting, 60 ethnic minority applicants each year were being denied the opportunity of an interview. Further, because of bias on interview, only 57% of ethnic minority interviewees were offered places, compared with 72% of white interviewees. In comparison, 37% of ethnic minority students were admitted through clearing, compared to 13% of white students (because clearing relied on examination results). Such issues of bias raise questions about the processes schools have in place for review of references and predictions, at least by a second person. Predictions should subsequently be reviewed against results to identify discrepancies and reasons for them.

The conclusion must be that training in this area, for those carrying responsibilities in relation to references and predictions, would be valuable in most schools.

CHAPTER 4

BULLYING

A particular concern for Governors is that pupils might complain that the school has been negligent in failing to prevent them from being bullied. Recent media coverage of suicides after being bullied and television documentaries on the subject have raised the profile of this issue with pupils and parents.

Schools are obviously concerned to eradicate bullying, to ensure the well-being of staff and pupils and to protect their reputation.

THE DfEE DEFINITION

Bullying is defined in paragraph 55 of DfEE Circular 8/94, "Pupil Behaviour and Discipline" as follows.

Bullying may be distinguished from other unacceptable forms of aggression in that it involves dominance of one pupil by another, or a group of others, is premeditated and usually forms a pattern of behaviour rather than an isolated incident. Many pupils experience bullying at some point. The fact that incidents have not been reported to staff does not mean they are not happening. Bullying or other forms of harassment can make pupils' lives unhappy, can hinder their academic progress and can sometimes push otherwise studious children into truancy. In extreme cases it can lead to pupils taking their own lives.

TAKING LEGAL ACTION

Reporting the Behaviour to the Police

A school bully could be held to have committed the offence of threatening behaviour under s.4 of the **Public Order Act 1986**, or be guilty of common assault or indecent assault.

Difficulties in Making a Criminal Complaint

Parents might be discouraged from making a complaint to the police for the following reasons:

- it may be difficult to proceed in a prosecution against a young child

- the parent must have evidence of what incident occurred, eg a doctor's report.

Judicial Review

If the school has failed to exclude a bully, the victim may bring an action in judicial review. Judicial review is only available when all rights of appeal against the school and the LEA have been exhausted. It is appropriate where the school or LEA failed to follow correct procedures or acted so unreasonably that no other school or LEA would have reached such a decision. The remedy is normally to order the school or the LEA to revisit the decision made, following the correct procedures. If the victim is seeking compensation for the injury he or she has suffered, an action for judicial review will not assist.

Negligence

In order for the victim to succeed in a claim of negligence, it is necessary to show that the Head owed a duty of care to the pupil which was breached by the Head failing to show the level of skill that would be expected of a reasonable member of the profession. Obviously, a school cannot guarantee absolute safety of its pupils and if the school did not know that bullying was taking place, the Head can hardly be said to have breached his or her duty of care to the child. The child will also need to demonstrate that the bullying caused the loss he or she is alleging, such as loss of confidence, career opportunities, etc. Very often, the loss alleged by the pupil has been caused by a number of factors, many of which may have been much more significant than the bullying at school. There may also be practical difficulties in the pupil actually providing any evidence that he or she suffered any damage at all.

In November 1996, a claim by a Sebastian Sharp, a former student of a school in south-west London, was settled out of court. The claim was that the school had failed to take steps that could reasonably be expected to prevent the constant bullying he suffered for a year. He claimed damages for the loss that he suffered as a result of the school's negligence, which allowed the bullying to take place. The loss claimed was his inability to obtain a well-paid job due to the fact that his schooling had suffered.

The case did not reach trial but the LEA's insurers made an out-of-court settlement of £30,000 rather than defend the claim. This is exceptional and a claim for damages for bullying has never been successful at trial. However, there is no doubt that a pupil who has been the victim of repeated bullying may well be able to prove loss. It seems reasonable that pupils should be compensated for the psychological damage that they have suffered from the school's failure to take appropriate action to prevent bullying. The cost of corrective therapy may well be quantifiable.

Walker v Derbyshire County Council (*The Times*, 7 June 1994) demonstrates that the bullying incidents must have been sufficiently distressing that a reasonable teacher could foresee psychiatric damage to the claimant. In this case, a girl was subjected to taunts, disapproving glares from the bullies and snide comments which she overheard at a 2-hour band practice over a 15-month period. Her claim that the school had been negligent in failing to stop the bullying was unsuccessful. The County Court held that the incidents complained of were not sufficiently distressing so that a reasonable teacher could foresee psychiatric damage to the claimant.

In the case of independent schools, there is no reason why the parents should not succeed in an action for a breach of contract if a child is bullied, and the school is aware of the bullying and fails to take any action to prevent it.

WHAT SCHOOLS CAN DO

Parents regularly report to the Children's Legal Centre, which publishes an information sheet on bullying, that some schools do not take bullying seriously enough. There are several reasons for this:

- teachers believe bullying is a normal and healthy part of school life
- the Head and parents may be unaware that the bullying is taking place (especially likely when the bullied child is too frightened to tell anyone what is happening)
- a teacher may not believe the bullied child when he or she does explain what is happening
- a teacher may fail to appreciate the seriousness of the complaint
- a teacher is bullying the child.

School Action

Research has shown that schools which adopted a clear anti-bullying stance experienced a 50% reduction in both *direct bullying* (open attacks on the victim) and *indirect bullying* (which includes isolating the victim and intentional exclusion from group activities). A whole-school approach is required for a clear anti-bullying stance to be adopted and this requires the involvement of all staff members, pupils and parents.

LEGAL REQUIREMENTS FOR SCHOOLS

Under s.38 in the **School Standards and Framework Act 1998** the overall responsibility for the conduct of the school is placed with the governing body. Section 61 of the Act goes on to make it clear that it is the duty of the governing body to ensure that there are policies designed to promote good behaviour and discipline and to ensure that these are pursued. After consulting with the Head and parents, the governing body has to make a general statement as to pupil discipline, setting out general principles to which the Head is to have regard. The governing body may also offer the Head guidance in relation to particular matters. The governing body is also under a duty to have regard to guidance (usually in the form of a Circular) given by the Secretary of State. This does not mean that the guidance has to be followed in every detail but a governing body will have to have very good and cogent reasons for any divergence. The Head is responsible for setting standards and determining disciplinary measures in line with the governing body's statement. The Head, having determined the necessary measures (which may include the making of rules and provision for enforcing them), must bring them to the attention of pupils, parents and staff every year. The measures should aim to:

- promote among pupils self-discipline and proper regard for authority

- encourage good behaviour and respect for others on the part of pupils and in particular prevent all forms of bullying among pupils

- ensure that the standard of behaviour of pupils is acceptable

- otherwise regulate the conduct of pupils.

The LEAs have reserve power to take such steps in relation to a maintained school as they consider are required to prevent the breakdown, or continuing breakdown of discipline at the school under s.62 of the **School Standards and Framework Act 1998**.

STEPS A SCHOOL SHOULD TAKE

DfEE Circulars should be considered (departmental circulars are not legally binding). It is however arguable that to the extent to which they give detailed professional guidance, the circulars do provide a guide for ascertaining what action a reasonable teacher should take. Circular 8/94, "Pupil Behaviour and Discipline" gives the advice listed below.

1. School staff must act (and be seen to act) firmly against bullying.

2. Policies on school behaviour and the associated rules of conduct should make specific reference to bullying.

3. Governing bodies should regularly review the school policy on bullying.

4. School prospectuses and other documents issued to parents and pupils should make it clear that bullying will not be tolerated.

5. School prospectuses should also give details of the arrangements by which bullied pupils can draw their concerns to the attention of staff, in the confidence that allegations will be carefully investigated and, if substantiated, taken seriously and acted on.

6. All members of staff must be alert to signs of bullying and act promptly and firmly against it — failure to respond to incidents may be interpreted as condoning the behaviour.

The priority is a whole-school approach with individual teachers responding to an incident.

The Head should make sure that the Circular has been drawn to the attention of members of staff and the governing body. The Head must also make sure that staff are aware of their day-to-day responsibilities to be alert to bullying and to act firmly against it.

Staff should be encouraged to report incidents to the head of the year and, if necessary, to the Head. If exclusion of a bully is considered, the Head should take into account the guidelines in DfEE Circular 10/94, "Exclusions from Schools".

Many schools have found that adopting an approach which encourages bullies to appreciate the effect of their actions on the victims has been very successful in reducing bullying in schools. It may be necessary for teachers to have specific training in leading this type of discussion.

RACIAL HARASSMENT

Similar considerations apply to racial harassment. The Commission for Racial Equality's definition is

> violence which may be verbal or physical and which includes attacks on property as well as on the person, suffered by individuals or groups because of their colour, race, nationality or ethnic origins, when the victim believes that the perpetrator was acting on racial grounds and/or there is evidence of racism.

It is important to remember that racial harassment does not happen only in schools with large ethnic minority populations.

DfEE Circular 8/94 gives the following advice:

1. To make it clear that it is viewed as a serious issue, schools should make explicit reference to racial bullying in their behaviour policies.
2. It should be made clear to pupils how they can bring any concerns they may have to the attention of the staff.
3. Staff should be alert to any emerging patterns of racial harassment.

SEXUAL HARASSMENT

Schools may want to make explicit reference in their behaviour policies to sexual harassment. DfEE Circular 8/94 contains the following advice:

1. Any incidents of sexual harassment should be taken seriously — and be seen to be taken seriously.
2. Schools should aim to encourage appropriate, responsible sexual behaviour, and to deter and address offensive behaviour. It may be most appropriate to address this in sex education classes.

INDEPENDENT SCHOOLS

Where there is a parent-school contract, it may be to the school's advantage to include a clause in the contract stating that parents who have cause for serious concern as to the care or safety of pupils should inform the Head without delay. This could prevent problems if parents are suing for breach of contract in a contractual action for the return of fees where it transpires that they have been aware of the problem for some time and have not brought it to the school's attention.

COMPLAINTS — PROCEDURE

The school should have some procedure for responding to written complaints. If a complaint is made to a class teacher, he or she should follow their school's policy which may require gathering as much information as possible regarding the dates, places and times of the alleged bullying and the names of the other children involved. Governors often appoint a sub-committee of three to five Governors to hear the complaint and determine what action should be taken. Parents are usually allowed to present evidence to the sub-committee. The Head or the person responsible for investigating the evidence is usually invited to give a report on the incidents complained of. The school should be able to produce a copy of its disciplinary policy to any parent making a complaint.

Lack of Appropriate Action

If parents feel that a school has not taken appropriate action, the parent of a child at an LEA-maintained school can make a complaint to the Director of Education via the LEA. The Director should respond to any complaint and can contact the school on a parent's behalf.

Parents can complain to the Local Government Ombudsman. The Ombudsman can only investigate complaints in a limited number of circumstances, ie when:

- the school or LEA has taken too long to take action without good reason
- the school has not followed its own rules or the law
- the school has given the wrong information or has not made a decision in the correct way.

If the Ombudsman decides to investigate, parents will be kept informed. A formal report is produced, which will say whether there has been maladministration by the LEA and/or by the school. The Ombudsman may recommend that compensation is paid or some other action taken to put things right. Most schools and LEAs comply with the Ombudsman's recommendations. The Ombudsman cannot force the school or LEA to pay compensation or comply with any other recommendations.

If all other complaint procedures have been exhausted, the last resort is a complaint to the Secretary of State for Education. If the Secretary of State is satisfied that the school has acted unreasonably, he or she may give such directions as appear expedient. However, it will be difficult for the parent to demonstrate this degree of failure on the part of the school and they may have to wait up to six months for a reply to their letter of complaint.

Withdrawing children from school

Some parents may choose to withdraw a bullied child from school and they have the right to deregister the child and educate him or her at home under s.7 of the **Education Act 1996**.

LEA Action in cases of Non-attendance or Partial Attendance

A bullied child might only be attending school part-time without the school's consent or not attending at all (and is not being educated at home). Governors need to be aware of what action is possible if the victim ceases to attend school.

Section19(1) of the **Education Act 1996** provides that the LEA has a duty to make full or part-time education provision for pupils who cannot attend school because of illness, exclusion or otherwise. If the parent is refusing to send the child to school, a medical or psychological assessment may be necessary to convince the LEA that the bullied child falls within this category.

The LEA can take steps to force a parent to make the child attend school, either through a school attendance order or an education supervision order.

School attendance order

A school attendance order may be served under s.437 of the **Education Act 1996** which requires the parent to register the child at the school named in the order if it appears that the child is not registered at school and is not receiving suitable education.

If parents fail to comply with a school attendance order, they can be prosecuted through the magistrates' court and may be fined. This can be counterproductive if the message conveyed is that not sending your child to school is roughly on a par with allowing a dog to foul the footpath.

Where the child *is* registered at a school, the LEA may decide to prosecute the parents if the child is not attending regularly, under s.444(1) of the **Education Act 1996**. Prosecution can result in a fine. There are a number of defences for parents prosecuted for this offence. If parents claim that they are keeping the child away because of illness, they would probably have to produce evidence to the court in the form of medical or psychological reports.

Education supervision order

The LEA, after consultation with Social Services, may also apply for an education supervision order if the child is not receiving a suitable education. A supervisor is appointed to advise, assist and befriend the child and parents, and to give directions to the parents to ensure that the child attends school. Failure to comply with a supervisor's directions is a criminal offence and can result in prosecution of the parents and a fine.

Clearly, however, bringing the parent before the court and a £50 fine will do little or nothing to improve the parent's self-esteem, or increase the motivation of the child. If family life is unsettled, or if there is violence, etc, regular attendance may be an unrealistic goal.

CONCLUSION

The message to Governors must be that an anti-bullying culture needs to be created at the school. Governors, because they have overall responsibility for discipline, must take responsibility for ensuring that policies which aim to deal with this issue are actually pursued. It is not sufficient to have a written policy — steps must be taken to monitor whether the policy is actually being implemented. If either the Head or the governing body have failed to comply with their statutory obligations or the recommendations of the Circular it will be easier for any victim of bullying to succeed in arguing that negligence occurred.

OTHER RELEVANT DfEE CIRCULARS

Other DfEE Circulars of relevance to Governors are listed below.

11/95: Misconduct of Teachers and Workers with Children and Young Persons

This Circular sets out the Secretary of State's powers to act in the cases of misconduct by teachers and other people who work with children.

10/95: Protecting Children from Abuse: The Role of the Education Service

This Circular gives guidance to teachers on their role in helping to protect children from abuse.

9/93: Protection of Children: Disclosure of Criminal Background of those with Access to Children

This Circular gives guidance about the arrangements for criminal background checks on people who are appointed to work with children.

10/98: Section 550A of the Education Act 1996: The Use of Force to Control or Restrain Pupils

This circular gives guidance as to the circumstances when it might be appropriate for teachers to intervene physically in a situation and discusses the meaning of reasonable force.

CHAPTER 5

PHYSICAL INJURY TO CHILDREN

INTRODUCTION

The roots of today's "litigation culture" lie in personal injury claims. In particular, the principal cases in the law of negligence have been concerned with identifying potential liability in circumstances where physical harm has been suffered as a consequence of another's action.

Accidents can happen anywhere — at home or at play, as much as at school or at work. The immediate reaction — to care for the injured — is the same everywhere. However, a secondary reaction is equally common if an accident occurs beyond the domestic setting — "who is liable?"

It is a common perception that if there has been an accident, then there is a concomitant liability on someone and that compensation might be available. Legal liability does not follow *every* incident in which people are injured or killed. The courts and legislators recognise that pure accidents really do happen. The purpose of this chapter is to discuss the nature of possible liabilities in this particular context. It also considers certain particular and topical examples.

BASES OF LIABILITY

Chapter 1 considered the distinction between:

- liability arising under the general law of negligence

- liability arising as a consequence of a failure to carry out some statutory function or requirement

- liability arising under a contract.

In the context of causing physical harm to pupils, the possibility of liability under *criminal* law should be mentioned. The deliberate infliction of physical harm would, in the absence of a lawful excuse, constitute an assault. Chastisement will not provide lawful excuse in the state sector, nor from 1 September 1999, assuming the coming into force of the relevant section of **School Standards and Framewrok Act 1998** in the dependent sector. (The offence would, incidentally, give rise to a seperate civil right of action for damages for the *tort* of assault.) Beyond that, if the action and the harm were so grave, lie the other caregories of violent offence, from assault occasioning grievous bodily harm through to corporate manslaughter.

Returning to the bases of potential civil liability, the following text discusses some of the key points.

Contracts — Definition and Exclusion of Liability

It is rare for any contract between school and parent to have any part in establishing the basis for potential liability. The contract will rarely say anything about the existence or standard of any duty of care that the school may have. However, this does not mean that the contract is not relevant.

For example, if the school stipulated (whether in "the contract" or via regulations or notices properly incorporated by reference — or indeed, outside the independent sector, in "one-off" arrangement letters) a required means of notification or registration of a child's known allergies and it was either followed or not followed, that might be relevant to the school's performance of its duty of care.

The contract might make it clear that a school bus service was not organised by the school but by third parties, with the effect that, once the formalities were completed to notify the school that a child could be committed to the service at the end of the school day, thereafter the school left matters between the parents and the third parties to deal with, for example, insurance and collection of the child at the dropping-off point.

The above examples show how the contract can be used to define the extent of responsibility. Clearly this could be abused, and responsibility that is actually undertaken could be "defined out" by the contract. However, it should be assumed that the courts will be astute and unsympathetic to such approaches.

What contract and notices cannot do is to exclude or restrict liability for physical harm or death under s.1 of the **Unfair Contract Terms Act 1977**. If the school has a legal responsibility, nothing in the contract can exclude or limit the extent of that responsibility.

Tort — Negligence

A teacher (and by reason of the application of "vicarious liability", the employer — see Chapter 1) owes a pupil a duty of care. The law recognises that the nature of their relationship, *in loco parentis*, is such as to give rise to a legal duty on the teacher to take all reasonable care to ensure the physical well-being of the pupil. There being such a duty, liability arises where the teacher does (or fails to do) something which might and does cause a foreseeable injury to the pupil. The application of this general principle is explored in particular cases later in this chapter. However, since "general principles" are of limited use *per se*, the following case study is an example of its application from within the education field (although the teacher's liability was not the point in issue by the time this particular case reached the Court of Appeal).

Mullin v Richards

Mullin v Richards [1998] 1 All ER 920 concerned a not untypical classroom game that ended in disaster. Two 15-year-old girls (the plaintiff and defendant) were "fencing" with plastic rulers during a mathematics lesson. In court, there was some disagreement as to whether it was a game in which they were both participating equally or whether it was a case of the plaintiff being baited by the defendant — the Court of Appeal thought the former was the case. In any event the defendant's ruler snapped, a piece of plastic entered the plaintiff's eye, blinding her in that eye.

There having been an accident, the plaintiff looked for someone to be liable. Besides the defendant, she also sued the LEA, the county council. However, the first instance judge decided that the teacher, whose lesson was coming to a close when the incident occurred, was not negligent — presumably there was nothing that she had done or not done which could be regarded as a breach of her general duty. Given that she gave evidence that the fencing game was known by her to take place and that she thought it was unacceptable; and also that the court found that the girls had not been told by anyone in the school not to play the game on the ground that it was potentially dangerous, this might seem slightly surprising, if pragmatic and slightly comforting from a school's point of view.

The judge found the other girl liable for the injury. The Court of Appeal disagreed. The main issue it decided related to the test to be applied when considering what a 15-year-old might be expected to foresee. For the purpose of this book, the case is intended to illustrate this "foreseeability" factor in negligence. The court decided that as there was no evidence of the game being played with dangerous force, it was not foreseeable that the ruler would break, splinter and cause such an injury.

The Court of Appeal emphasised its sympathy for the plaintiff, who had suffered a grave injury through no fault of her own, but as the judge said, "she has failed to establish...that anyone was legally responsible for that injury."

While it is true that the boundaries of the law of negligence are not closed and also true that the defendant in this case had to take a case to the Court of Appeal to succeed, it is equally true that the law is tending to approach novel or borderline claims with a degree of robustness which may be disguised by the statement of "the general principle" but which is exemplified in the *Mullin* case.

Statutory Duties

The mandatory requirements imposed by the **Health and Safety at Work Act 1974** and its associated regulations apply to schools with as much rigour as any other place of work. The "employer", be it the LEA, the governing body, the employing trust, or the proprietor, is under a duty to ensure that the health and safety of not only those in their employment, ie teachers and all other members of staff, but also those affected by the undertaking, ie pupils.

Although breach of statutory duty is the stick, it is the personal element which makes it important that there is an effective management system in place to ensure the health and safety of all teachers, other members of staff, and the pupils. The "employer" is under a duty to ensure that there is sound planning, implementation, monitoring, and reviewing of health and safety procedures. If the guidelines set out in *Managing Health and Safety in Schools* produced by the Education Service Advisory Committee are followed, there should be no difficulty in complying with their legal duty.

While no similar guidlines can be referred to, the duties of the "occupier" of premises (including school premises) towards those present on those premises are provided by the **Occupiers' Liability Act 1957**. In effect, this requires a level of responsibility (the "common duty of care") with regard to the condition of the premises and activities carried out on them which is almost the same as that under the general law of negligence.

NEGLIGENCE LIABILITY — SPECIFIC EXAMPLES

Sporting Injuries

In general terms, the issue of liabilities arising in the course of sporting activities is in a process of reassessment. The orthodox position has been that in most cases where injury occurs, so long as it was not caused by a deliberate and calculated foul, then nobody (neither opposite player, nor referee, nor his or her employer) was legally responsible. This is not because of the absence of a right of action (whether for negligence or assault) but because the injured party (even a child) was considered to have consented to the degree of bodily contact, even accidental contact, necessary incidental to the playing of the game; or, in other sports, to have consented to the degree of risk inherent in the activity. This is the rule of law known as *volenti non fit injuria* (no wrong is done to someone who consents).

However, even this summary indicates that there were limits placed by the courts on the freedom of sportsmen, or those operating, organising or training sports, to carelessly inflict harm on one another. When might the fateful action exceed that normally to be expected in a game, or when might a player be acting deliberately rather than negligently?

This is the area in which the law is developing. It does not do so alone. Sports and sporting activities are themselves developing to recognise and manage risk. Where this is the case, the law follows. However, it does so with an eye for the general benefit of allowing and encouraging sport.

In the well-known case of *Smolden v Whitworth*, a rugby referee was found liable in negligence when a front-row forward sustained a catastrophic spinal injury in a colts match which he was refereeing.

The decision shocked those involved in sports organisation, particularly within the education sector. However, the facts of the case and the comments of the Court of Appeal deserve close scrutiny to explain why the case, though significant and a warning, should be of application to most cases of sporting injury.

Two particularly important facts were that up to the point when the plaintiff was injured in a collapsed scrum, there had been 20 collapsed scrums, and that the Rugby Football Union had recognised the risks of very serious spinal injury created by scrums and in 1991 had reviewed the laws of the game to try and ensure that, at the junior level of rugby, the scrums were managed in a way which most avoided the risk.

The evidence showed that the referee had not applied the new rules and had not taken the very straightforward precautions which he should have known about to control the teams' scrums. He was, therefore, in breach of the duty he owed the players.

However, the court emphasised that it recognised that rugby was a physical game in which minor injury was expected, and that a referee had to apply the rules, through split-second decision-making, in a way in which both discouraged dangerous play and allowed the game to flow. The court was clear that it would judge a referee's actions in the light of all of these factors and, while finding the referee liable, made the point that "the threshold of liability was a high one [which] would not easily be crossed".

Schools should ensure that staff who have charge of such matters receive relevant and regular training .

Health Risks

In 1986 (this date is relevant), a school was aware that a 16-year-old girl suffered from asthma. During a lesson, she began to exhibit signs of breathing difficulty but declined her teacher's suggestion that she should go home. Less than 30 minutes later, the girl's inhaler was not improving the condition and the teacher gave her a note for the school secretary. On leaving the warm classroom, the cold air in the corridor made her condition worse and she collapsed. It took her 20 minutes to take a route to the secretary's office that would normally take one minute. A few minutes later she collapsed and suffered severe brain damage. Was the school liable in this case?

Certainly the school owed a duty of care. That duty was specific in relation to the girl's asthma. The court was surprised by the LEA's suggestion that it owed no duty to get medical help for a pupil over 16 — however, it may be assumed that there *is* such a duty.

However, the school was not liable. While there was no positive evidence that the school had told the teacher of the pupil's condition, the court was not convinced that the knowledge would have altered her reaction to events. The critical issue then was foreseeability — in particular whether the teacher should have known that there was a risk of serious injury in the events that occurred. The court thought she should not — but (and it is a big "but") emphasised that it was judging against the state of knowledge of asthma in 1986. Then (although possibly not now), it was reasonable for the teacher not to have realised that the delay and the sudden exposure to cold would have worsened the condition and increased the risk of a serious incident.

Expeditions and Excursions — Out-of-hours and Off-premises

The potential for liability arising from adventure activities and other out-of-school outings raises much the same considerations as discussed under *Sporting Injuries* on page 59.

One may anticipate that, dealing with young people and dangerous activities, the courts will expect a standard of behaviour from the organiser which is somewhat higher than it might from a teacher in a classroom or with an event for adults. In a well-publicised case, a mountain guide whose actions led to the death of his adult client was found to be liable. Cases arising from the Lyme Bay canoeing incident are also relevant.

Schools often contract out the organisation of such activities. Provided it can be shown that in selecting a provider, the school took all reasonable care in making that selection, it is likely that the scope for any remaining liability will be vastly reduced.

For other "non-adventurous" out-of-school activities, the law will apply a similar standard as to school activities — judging compliance by reference to the facts at the time.

What is the position for non-authorised out-of-school activity, eg where a pupil plays truant and is hurt? It will depend on the facts but it is likely that the plaintiff will face some difficulty in establishing liability. In *Nwabudike v Southwark LBC* (The Times, 28 June 1996), a primary school pupil was run over at lunchtime. The school showed that he was determined to abscond and that the school's record was generally very good — there had been only one similar incident of a child leaving the school in six years. The court felt that it should balance the need to ensure safety with the need to avoid a "siege mentality" and decided that the school had taken all reasonable care.

Intruders

Following the incidents of Dunblane and Wolverhampton, what must a school do to satisfy its legal duty to protect the safety of children from intruders? The issue is better and more frequently put as a practical one rather than a legal one, ie "what can we do?" There is a reasonable chance that the answers will be the same.

The law's approach, in common with its approach to each specific example considered in this chapter, will be to assess what the school knew or ought to have known of the risks, and the reasonableness of its response. The response will vary from school to school. A large country-based school with large grounds might reasonably decide to implement certain controls (eg visitor passes, close security in specific areas, etc), while an inner-city primary school might reasonably implement others (eg high fences and entryphones). Two schools in the same environment with similar physical surroundings might well reach different conclusions as to what they will do, taking into account their own risk assessments and other priorities.

What may be important should liability ever become an issue (and this is of wider application than this example alone) is that the school has some record of its appraisal of the risks and the reasons for its particular response. The cases will be few where, faced with the evidence of a researched and thought-through decision, a judge decides that he or she is better placed to second-guess the view reached.

CHAPTER 6

LIABILITY ARISING FROM SUBSTANCE ABUSE

INTRODUCTION

For the purpose of this chapter, the term "substance abuse" is taken to mean the use and abuse not only of illegal drugs but also alcohol and other legal substances that lend themselves to abuse — particularly those described as "volatile substances". Substance abuse is a universal problem. DfEE Circular 4/95 "Drug Prevention and Schools" states:

> Drug misuse is as much an issue for schools in rural areas and affluent communities as for disadvantaged inner city areas. There are no "no go areas" for illegal drugs. Drug misuse extends across socio-economic and ethnic boundaries. Educationally successful young people are just as likely to find themselves at risk. No school can afford to be complacent or to think its pupils are not at risk.

Other than to note that in this area, as in others, schools reflect society, the primary concern of this chapter is the legal issues rather than the social or educational issues. Criminal law relating to drugs, alcohol and other substances are summarised, then consideration is given to how a school might acquire a civil liability arising out of substance abuse.

CRIMINAL LAW

Illegal Drugs

Illegal drugs are those classified under the **Misuse of Drugs Act 1971** as "controlled drugs". The Act creates the following relevant offences:

- to supply, or offer to supply, a controlled drug (other than in accordance with the procedures created by the 1971 Act)

- to be in possession of, or to possess with the intent to supply to another, a controlled drug

- for the occupier or someone concerned in the management of any premises knowingly to permit or suffer on those premises the smoking of cannabis or the production, supply, or offering to supply of any controlled drug.

The Act provides that an offence is not committed where someone is in possession of what he or she knows or suspects to be a controlled drug if:

- they took possession of it in order to prevent another person committing an offence or continuing to commit an offence, *and*

- as soon as possible after taking possession of it, they take all steps reasonably open to them to either destroy the drug or to deliver it into the custody of the police or some other person lawfully entitled to take custody of it.

This is an important safeguard for teachers.

In the exercise of its normal disciplinary or pastoral function, a school may enquire into alleged or suspected cases of drug offences (whether contrary to the **Misuse of Drugs Act 1971** or to school rules).

The DfEE advises that a school is permitted to search a pupil's desk or locker where it has reasonable cause to believe it contains unlawful items including illegal drugs. This is probably implied in the nature of the school-pupil relationship. Where the opportunity exists to provide expressly for such a right (usually only available in the independent school sector, through the contract with parents) it should be considered. It should be under a broad right of investigation into disciplinary offences and not limited to cases involving drugs.

However, in the absence of a consent from the pupil, the school is not permitted to search the pupil. To do so would risk committing an assault. If a pupil declines to co-operate in any enquiry, the school should consider calling in the police who will conduct any investigation under the **Police and Criminal Evidence Act 1984** and its associated Codes of Practice.

Alcohol and Tobacco

The law on the sale of alcohol is governed by the **Licensing Act 1964**. Under this Act it is, for example, an offence to sell intoxicating liquor without a licence or to sell alcohol to anyone under 18.

It is an offence to give any child under the age of five intoxicating liquor under s.5 of the **Children and Young Persons Act 1933**.

Similarly, it is an offence to sell cigarettes to a child under the age of 16 under s.1 of the **Children and Young Persons (Protection from Tobacco) Act 1991**.

Volatile Substances

There is no law against the possession or sale of volatile substances, expect that it is an offence to supply a substance to someone aged under 18 "knowing or having reasonable cause to believe that the substance or its fumes are likely to be used by that person for the purpose of causing intoxication" **(Intoxicating Substances (Supply) Act 1985)**.

Schools' Responsibilities in Relation to Criminal Offences

Apart from any criminal liability of its own which might arise under the provisions outlined above, where does a school stand when it has reason to believe that an offence has been committed by somebody else — particularly a pupil?

The school may have a number of reasons why it does not wish to involve the police — pastoral care being the most common. In many cases, schools have followed DfEE advice and have established a means of liaison with local police, which may include provision for a way of dealing with such cases short of formal police involvement. Where this is not the case, the school is not legally required to report suspicions or even offences. However, the DfEE makes it clear that it would expect schools to do so.

CIVIL LIABILITY

The following text considers the school's potential exposure to civil claims relating to substance abuse and to means adopted by many schools (particularly or even solely, in the independent sector) as part of their response to the problem, eg testing for drugs.

Liability Generally

The question here is whether a school's response to substance abuse generally or specifically to any child might give grounds for liability. It will be very rare that a claim arises in a direct fashion. However, it is important to bear in mind the actions that have been commenced which allege that schools failed to deal adequately with matters such as bullying, special educational needs or health requirements. While the courts will scrutinise any claim very closely — and, at the time of writing, it is rare for the plaintiff to succeed — it is possible that the run of the legal tide will change.

Areas of Risk

Theoretically, the following are areas of risk.

Failure to provide adequate education

A pupil might argue that the school failed to provide adequate education in relation to substance abuse generally. In response, the school should be able to defend its position if it has taught those elements of the national curriculum which touch on these areas of personal and social development, and that, in its education approach, it has taken into account the particular factors peculiar to its own situation.

Failure to respond to individual needs

A pupil might argue that the school failed to respond to his or her particular needs in a reasonable manner. If the pupil was a user of substances, he or she might argue that the school was too lenient on him or her and other offenders, or alternatively, that the school was too strict.

In the state sector, schools are encouraged to develop and maintain a policy towards substance abuse and abusers. This may include a statement of the disciplinary approach that the school might take. While recognising that exclusion may be an appropriate response to immediate circumstances in some cases, the DfEE discourages permanent exclusion as the usual recourse. In the case of liability, what is likely to be important is that a policy is in place and that it is adhered to.

In the independent sector, HMC has recommended that its members also develop policies in relation to substance abuse — especially illegal drugs. Again, a statement of the disciplinary consequences of committing an offence or breaching school rules is usually an integral part of such policies. Some schools have thought it appropriate to make expulsion an automatic consequence of offending; others have reserved that power for serious cases, while offering in other cases a more pastoral approach through "contracts" and random testing for drug use (see page 71).

Contractual claims

In the independent sector, perhaps particularly with boarding schools, either of the two arguments outlined above is sometimes raised as a contractual claim by the child's parents. This usually follows an expulsion in an effort to have the Governors reassess their claims for reinstatement or as a counterclaim for unpaid fees. For example, where a child is expelled for vandalism following a drinking binge, the parents may claim that the root of the problem was the school's attitude to alcohol and its failure to monitor their child sufficiently closely. The school's best response is to review its educational and social approaches to alcohol as taught to this child (pointing if possible to published material explaining that to parents) and, very importantly, show that it took every reasonable step in investigating the offence, so as to comply with the requirements of a fair hearing.

The advantages of having policies in place is that they will indicate to a court that the school has considered the problem and, provided (and it is an important proviso) the school's actions are in accordance with the policy's provisions, it will be very rare that a court would wish to second-guess the school's conclusions as to what is appropriate in its circumstances.

Other Areas of Liability

There are other possible areas of liability that one might devise but require only brief mention. It is conceivable that someone injured by contact on school grounds with discarded syringes or other material connected with drug abuse (which may have no connection with the school apart from the use of its land by drug users) might have a claim against the school if the school had not taken reasonable care to minimise the risk (which will require the school to have some knowledge of the problem). A third party who is injured, or whose property was damaged by intoxicated pupils might have a claim against the school under the usual tort of negligence if it could be established that the school knew enough about the likelihood of a problem so that the damage was foreseeable and failed to take reasonable precautions. Similarly, if a school turns a blind eye to a pupil possessing or trafficking drugs, claim may be brought against it for putting other students at risk.

DRUG TESTING

Following HMC's recommendation that schools develop policies towards drug abuse, many independent schools decided to regularise their approach to the problem. "Regularising" meant such features as:

- a clear statement, in the contractual papers, of the school's disciplinary policy (whether it is immediate expulsion, or a "flexible response")

- the use of targeted drugs tests to "prove" guilt or innocence

- the offer of random tests after an offence has been committed to monitor a period of "rehabilitation".

Each element renders the school's approach more formal, more capable of being proven, should a decision be challenged or a claim brought.

Without doubt, revisiting and revising both contract and procedure is likely to reduce a school's exposure to claims by parents arising from expulsions — assuming of course that the school sticks to both the contract and the procedure. It is too much to believe that that exposure will be negated entirely. Given the publicity accorded to possible flaws in the forensic reliability of drug-test results in tests on athletes, dissatisfied parents might acquire a new means of attack.

What then are the key areas of exposure to risk to claims and how might the school prepare for them?

Contract Terms

Clear wording to describe the availability of the ultimate sanction coupled with as clear as possible a description of the area of discretion left to the Head should reduce the exposure to claims that he or she went beyond his or her powers in expelling a pupil.

Contract Procedures

Most contracts leave matters of discipline and punishment to the Head. Some — sometimes for reasons that seem to be historic — require a

71

degree of liaison with Governors. The rule is, whatever the procedure, comply with it.

This rule applies equally to the evidence-gathering stage. It may be debatable whether the procedures for the carrying out of the drugs tests will have contractual force (perhaps because of the timing of amendments to contract terms and uncertainty over the power to issue unilateral notices altering those terms). On the other hand, the procedures simply reflect requirements of natural justice. It is a practical fact that having stipulated the procedures in advance, often having distributed those procedures to parents or offered them for inspection, failure to follow them will give at least the basis of a complaint, and that is undesirable. More seriously, while urine testing is non-invasive and would not amount to an assault, the school needs to be satisfied that the child and parents have at some stage:

– consented to the procedure

– understand what it entails and its consequences.

Test Results

In most cases, the testing will be out of the school's hands, certainly from the time that the sample is packaged. The school should be satisfied that its choice of laboratory is a reasonable one. It must ensure that the procedures for which it is responsible are adhered to. It must be clear what the results mean when they are received, especially the degree to which they can reasonably be regarded as "conclusive". Drug users, drug testers and test challengers are each developing their particular skills at pace. It will not be possible for any school to be certain that it understands the state of the art at any particular point — it must act on advice. Preferably (and unlike the provisions in most sports' rulebooks) test results will be but one element leading to a sanction.

Procedure

A common ground for attacking a school's decision is failure to follow fair procedures. It is a fact that most, if not all, schools will be anxious to avoid unfairness when dealing with any pupil. It is beyond the scope of this chapter to discuss the requirements of a fair hearing (and while the theory still holds that an independent school is not (usually) a public body susceptible to the remedies afforded by judicial review, that theory is beginning to break down and may suffer further erosion when the **Human Rights Act 1998** comes into force). Briefly, but which cannot be too strongly emphasised, it is important to document every step of the proceedings, from collation of teachers' observations, through initial form teachers' interviews, references to the Head, notification of testing to child and parents and throughout, even after the event. Parents will make much of representations held out but not honoured, of unfair pressure applied, etc. Paper evidence gives a chance of countering these points early in any litigation process.

CHAPTER 7

ADMISSIONS AND EXCLUSIONS

The Government's reforms mean that parents can express a preference for the school they wish their child to attend (s.86 **School Standards and Framework Act 1998**) and give reasons for their preference. The parents must have that preference met unless all the places have already been offered to children with stronger claims. Parents have access to information about schools and school performance and have the right to appeal to an independent committee if their child is refused a place.

ADMISSION AUTHORITIES

Type of School

Each school has its own admission authority. The identity of the admission authority depends upon the type of school.

County schools
The admissions policy of county schools is usually dictated by the LEA.

Voluntary aided schools

The governing body will agree its admissions policy with the LEA. The policy can include criteria that are intended to preserve the distinctive character of the school. Most often, this relates to religious qualifications for entry to denominational schools.

Grant-maintained schools

Schools will have indicated their admissions policy in their initial proposals for grant-maintained status which the Secretary of State will have approved. Grant-maintained schools are free to change their admissions policy without the consent of the Secretary of State, provided that the change does not involve significant change to the character of the school. The Secretary of State had previously taken the view that a "significant change of character" will, in general, result from the admission of up to 10% of pupils on the basis of ability or aptitude in one or more of music, art, drama, sport, technology and foreign languages. DfEE Circular 6/96 "Admissions to Maintained Schools" made it clear that the Secretary of State considered that selection of up to 15% of the school's intake in any subject or combination of subjects or by general ability was possible without the need to publish statutory proposals.

New school categories

When the new school categories come into being, the admission authority in relation to a foundation or voluntary aided school will be the school's governing body. In relation to a community or voluntary controlled school, the admission authority will be the LEA or the governing body where, with the governing body's agreement, the LEA have delegated to them responsibility for determining the admission arrangements for the school.

Admission Criteria

Admission arrangements, including the criteria by which decisions are to be made if a school is oversubscribed, must be published annually in the school's prospectus. LEAs and schools should make every effort to ensure that these arrangements are clearly and accurately described.

Co-ordination

Parents have the right to apply for more than one school at the same time. Obviously, in an area with a number of different admission authorities, a co-ordinated approach is of benefit to parents and to the authorities themselves.

Duty to Comply with Parental Preference

The admission authority — whether it is the LEA or the governing body — is under similar obligations to comply with parental preference. Existing legislation relating to the obligation to comply with parental preference and the circumstances in which it is permitted not to do so is to be re-enacted. An application must be accepted unless:

– admission would be incompatible with any arrangements for preserving the particular religious character of the school or any arrangements for selecting pupils by reference to ability or aptitude

– admissions would prejudice the provisions of efficient education or the efficient use of resources of the school.

In determining whether prejudice exists, the school must have regard to its published admissions limit.

Operating an Admissions Policy

The DfEE Circular explains that admission authorities must act lawfully and reasonably when considering applications for school places. The criteria for oversubscription must not be unreasonable. The courts will regard as unreasonable admissions criteria which no sensible authority acting with due appreciation of its responsibilities would have decided to adopt. It is interesting that the Circular makes clear that school places may not be offered subject to the signing of a home-school contract.

Moreover, once an offer of a school place has been made, only in very limited circumstances may an admission authority lawfully withdraw that offer.

SCHOOL STANDARDS AND FRAMEWORK ACT 1998

The **School Standards and Framework Act 1998** sets out extensive provisions relating to admissions policies for foundation, voluntary and community schools.

The Act reflects the Government's determination to rationalise the admissions process. Admission authorities will be required to consult on admission arrangements each year and provide a method of resolving local disputes. The legislation relating to admissions will come into force for the admission round in the year 1999/2000.

When the provisions of the new Act come into force, the LEA will be the admission authority for community and voluntary controlled schools unless this has been delegated by agreement to the governing body, while the governing bodies of voluntary aided and foundation schools will be their own admission authorities.

Each admission authority will be required to determine its admission arrangements each year and before doing so to consult with, in effect, all admission authorities within the locality. The LEA must also consult with the schools for whom it is the admission authority. Where there is to be a change during the year, the admission authority must refer the proposal to the adjudicator who has the sole power to decide whether they should be implemented.

It will still be possible for the governing bodies of foundation or voluntary aided schools to make arrangements in respect of the admission of pupils to the school to preserve the religious character of the school. If the LEA does not agree to proposals by the governing body, they may be included in the draft, which is subject to consultation but must be referred to the adjudicator or the Secretary of State. The adjudicator will be appointed by the Secretary of State in accordance with regulations and subject to supervision by the Council of Tribunals. The adjudicator may decide that the proposals are to be adopted or may refer the question to the Secretary of State.

The main change to the provisions relating to the admission authority's power to fix the admission number for any relevant age group and any school year at not less than the relevant standard number is the duty of the LEA and governing body to comply with the limit on infant class sizes.

Section 99 of the **School Standards and Framework Act 1998** prohibits admission by reference to ability unless the school is a grammar school or the form of selection is a permitted one, namely one of those set out in s.99(2) as:

- any selection by ability authorised by s.100 (pre-existing arrangements)

- any selection by ability authorised by s.101 (pupil banding)

- any selection by ability conducted in connection with the admission of pupils to the school for secondary education suitable to the requirements of pupils who are over compulsory school age.

The section also prohibits admission by reference to aptitude unless the form of selection is a permitted one, namely pre-existing arrangements or selection by aptitude for particular subjects as authorised by s.102.

Very briefly, therefore, when the new Act comes into force, schools which partially select will be able to continue to do so but the co-ordination of admissions should make it more difficult for parents to hold several offers.

The DfEE has produced interim guidance to admission authorities on school admissions. This will be superseded early next year by a new statutory Admissions Code of Practice, copies of which can be obtained from the DfEE Publications Centre, PO Box 5050, Sudbury, Suffolk CO10 6ZQ. The principles promoted in this guidance should be borne in mind by Governors when drafting their admissions guidelines:

- meeting parental preference

- openness, fairness and objectivity in admissions criteria
- the need for local consultation and for co-ordinated, common local arrangements for the benefit of parents
- discontinuance of partial selection by ability where it is operating in a way which is against the interests of the children of the area.

APPEALS AGAINST REFUSALS TO ADMIT

Parents have the right to appeal to an appeal committee against a refusal to admit their child. The way in which an appeal committee approaches admission issues has been laid out in a Code of Practice. The appeal committee must first consider whether the admission authority has no duty to comply with the parent's preference because to admit another child would prejudice the provision of efficient education or efficient uses of resources. If the admission authority fails to satisfy the committee of prejudice, the committee must allow the appeal and allocate the child a place at the school. If, however, the committee is satisfied that prejudice would arise, it must then decide if the reasons given by the parents for their preference are sufficient to outweigh the prejudice that would result. The decision of the appeal committee must be given in writing.

The **School Standards and Framework Act 1998** will not bring a huge amount of change to the way in which appeals are dealt with — appeals in respect of community and voluntary controlled schools will be arranged by the LEA. Appeals in respect of voluntary aided and foundation schools will be arranged by the school's governing body.

The provision enacted in the **Education Act 1997** (which does not allow the parent an appeal where a place is refused to an applicant who has been permanently excluded from two schools where at least one of those exclusions was after 1 September 1997) is re-enacted but the governing body of a school to whom such a child has been admitted by the LEA acting as admission authority is given a right of appeal against that decision.

Schedule 24 of the new Act sets out how the appeal panel will be constituted. In all cases, the appeal panel will consist of three or five members and will be a mixture of lay people and people with experience in education. The appeal panel should not consist of people who may be perceived to be biased so it will not be permissible for a member of the LEA or a member of the governing body to be a member of the panel.

Relevant Cases

The judicial approach to this subject is best illustrated by recent cases.

R v The Governors of La Sainte Union Convent School, ex parte T

In *R v The Governors of La Sainte Union Convent School, ex parte T* [1996] ELR 98, T's father applied for her to enter La Sainte Union Convent School, a Roman Catholic school. The application was refused because the family had failed to establish their Catholicity and the girl's suitability for the religious ethos of the school. However, leave was granted to challenge the rejection by the school of the admission of T because no regard was had to the mother's religion. This was because the mother and father had been divorced for a long time and there appeared to be no contact between the mother and daughter. T had, however, been baptised into the Roman Catholic church as a baby and this was very unusual when neither parent was a practising Roman Catholic.

The judge observed that if a publicly funded school with statutory permission adopts an exclusionary rule which shuts out many children who may live nearby and want to go to the school on religious grounds then it must expect it to be strictly construed. Therefore, leave to apply for judicial review was granted.

R v Education Appeal Committee of Leicestershire County Council, ex parte Tarmohamed

In *R v Education Appeal Committee of Leicestershire County Council, ex parte Tarmohamed* [1996] COD 286 (QBD), Tarmohamed's appeal to the appeal committee for his daughter to attend a particular school was unsuccessful. The court held that the correct procedure had been followed by the committee. It had concluded that there would be prejudice to the provision of efficient education or the efficient use of resources if additional pupils were admitted to the school and it had then considered in turn each case to see if parental preference could be granted.

R v Essex County Council, ex parte Jacobs

The parent in *R v Essex County Council, ex parte Jacobs* [1997] 2 ELR 190 expressed a preference for twins to attend the same school as their two older siblings. The school was the most convenient for both parents who were divorced and lived outside the catchment area. The parent also argued that he wanted all his children to attend the same school. The school had reached its standard number with children whose parents lived in the catchment area. Any additional places had been allocated to children whose siblings attended the school and on the basis of nearness to the family home. The parent appealed to the appeal committee alleging that additional places had been allocated to children who lived outside the catchment area and had no siblings at the school.

The parent was successful in seeking judicial review of the decision. The committee had to carry out a two-stage process. It first had to decide whether there would be prejudice to the efficient provision of education and use of resources if any extra pupil were admitted. It then had to undertake a balancing exercise if there were circumstances sufficiently exceptional as to outweigh the prejudice which an extra pupil is deemed to cause.

The evidence indicated that the committee *did* fail to have regard to all the relevant circumstances. It may well not have attached sufficient weight to the matters which were being put forward on behalf of the applicant as amounting to special circumstances to outweigh the prejudice to efficient education. There was unfairness to the applicant and the decisions of the appeal committee would have to be quashed and sent back for fresh consideration.

R v Wiltshire County Council, ex parte Razazan

In *R v Wiltshire County Council, ex parte Razazan* [1997] 3 ELR 370 CA, a child who lived in Somerset was denied a place at an oversubscribed school in Wiltshire. After an unsuccessful application for judicial review, the child appealed. The parents alleged that Wiltshire's LEA decision was unlawful as s.6 of the **Education Act 1980** (now s.411 of the **Education Act 1996**) required those living inside and outside an LEA's area to be treated equally in terms of preference for a school. The court was in complete agreement with the conclusion reached by Popplewell J in the instant case and was in equal agreement with his stated reasons.

It held that it was clear that Wiltshire had adopted reasonable criteria in order to determine those applications of an oversubscribed school which would be accepted and those which would be rejected. There was no discrimination against those resident outside the county.

R v Rotherham Metropolitan Borough Council, ex parte Clark and Others

In *R v Rotherham Metropolitan Borough Council, ex parte Clark and Others* (The Times, 20 November 1997, CA), the LEA had a policy of allocating places in its secondary schools through the use of catchment areas. Prospective parents who lived within the catchment area for a particular school were told by letter that their child would be allocated a place automatically. It was argued that these parents did not exercise any preference. They were told that if they did nothing, their child was allocated to the catchment area school. The result was that many places available at the relevant school were filled up before those expressing a true preference for the school could have their opinion considered. Parents who wished to send their children to a particular school despite their living outside its catchment area were allocated any remaining places by such criteria as distance from the school and whether there was a sibling already there. The applicants were all parents who lived outside the catchment area for the Old Hall School and had been refused places there for their children.

The judge held that the policy of the LEA was unlawful. In order to follow the dictates of Parliament it was essential that an LEA, before it allocated places, knew what the preferences were even from those within the catchment area.

Conclusion

The following points emerge:

- admission policies may be strictly construed

- an appeal committee must follow procedure carefully and in an unbiased way

- parents must be given the right to express a preference.

It is hoped that increased co-ordination between admission authorities might reduce the number of appeals when the **School Standards and Framework Act 1998** is implemented, but how the arrangements will work in practice remains to be seen.

EXCLUSIONS FROM SCHOOL

DfEE Circular 10/94 "Exclusions from School" sets out the guiding principles that should govern the use of exclusions as a sanction by schools. The Circular makes it clear that unless other suitable arrangements are made, all pupils should be in school and learning. Exclusions are only appropriate in response to serious breaches of the school's policy on behaviour or of criminal law. It is not an appropriate response to every form of behavioural difficulty.

Permanent exclusions should be used sparingly and only after other strategies have failed. In short, it is a *last resort* and appropriate only when allowing the child to remain in school would be seriously detrimental to the education or welfare of the pupil or to that of other pupils.

Types of Exclusion

An exclusion must either be:

– for a fixed period *or*

– permanent.

The power to exclude for an indefinite period was abolished in 1993, as it was felt that indefinite exclusion sometimes led to exclusions lasting longer than warranted and inherently involved a large amount of uncertainty for the child and parents.

Fixed-period exclusions

A fixed-period exclusion is for a specified period. The former limit of up to 15 school days in any one term was changed by the **Education Act 1997** to a limit of not more than 45 school days in any one school year. It is not expected, however, that a Head would use all of the fixed period in one exclusion. An initial fixed period lasting from two to five days should normally enable the Head to make sufficient investigations as to the nature of the incident leading to the exclusions. If necessary, this period can be extended to allow time for further reports or supportive work with the pupils or parents.

Permanent exclusion

A pupil who is permanently excluded from school is removed from the school roll once the exclusion is confirmed and any appeal has been dealt with.

The Role of the Head and Governing Body

The Circular makes clear the role of the Head, the governing body and the LEA in the exclusion procedure.

The Role of the Head

Only the Head has power to exclude a child (or, exceptionally, a deputy head acting in the Head's absence). The Circular makes clear that where the recommendation for exclusion comes from a teacher, the Head must wait until he or she is in possession of all the relevant facts and has firm evidence to support the allegations made. In the interests of fairness, this should include an opportunity for the pupil facing exclusion to express a view.

It is only appropriate for a decision to be taken in the heat of the moment where there is an immediate risk to the safety of the pupil or other pupils or staff.

How Governors can support the Head and staff

Governors can support the Head and staff in maintaining high standards of discipline and ensuring fairness to individual pupils and their parents. DfEE Circular 10/94 states that

> any punishment should be appropriate to offence and that each instance of poor behaviour needs to be examined individually and in the context of established school behaviour policies and in the light of criminal law.

The Circular makes clear that exclusions should only be used after due consideration of the personal circumstances of the child and the incident itself, for example the degree of severity of the behaviour, the frequency of its occurrence and the likelihood of it recurring. Another relevant factor is whether or not the behaviour occurred on school premises or when the pupil was in the charge of school staff. If the incident occurred off school premises, an important consideration is the extent to which behaviour away from the school had a serious impact on the life of the school.

The Circular draws attention to circumstances where exclusions might be inappropriate, including the following situations.

- The behaviour may be an emerging sign of an emotional and behavioural difficulty.

- The school simply does not have sufficient resources to cope with the child's particular behaviour. In these circumstances, the Head should discuss the problem with the governing body and the LEA.

- Pupils cannot comply with uniform or dress regulations for cultural or religious reasons. Exclusion might constitute unlawful indirect discrimination under the **Race Relations Act 1976**.

- The pupil is being treated as a scapegoat. It is important to consider whether the incident was perpetrated by the pupil alone or as part of a group.

- A home-school agreement has been broken. Home-school agreements have no legal basis. They are voluntarily entered into after the child has been awarded a place and should not be included in the school's admissions criteria. It is important simply to consider whether the particular offence warrants exclusion.

- The incident is trivial, for example failure to complete homework or bring dinner money.

- The pupil has not been attending school. Exclusion in these circumstances could hinder effective action to tackle unauthorised absence.

- The pupil is pregnant.

Voluntary Withdrawals

The Circular actively discourages Heads from putting pressure on parents to withdraw their children from school voluntarily. This is because such pressure denies the pupil and parent the safeguards of access to the permanent exclusion procedures and appeal mechanisms to which they may be entitled.

PROCEDURES

Fixed-period Exclusions

The current procedure differs slightly depending on the type of school.

County, voluntary and maintained special schools

The key aspects are as follows. The Head must inform the pupil's parents of:

– the exclusion

– the duration of the exclusion

– sufficient particulars to ensure the reason for the exclusion is fully understood and all relevant circumstances made known.

If the exclusion is for more than five days or involves the loss of opportunity to take a public examination, or the period of exclusion has reached an aggregate of more than five days in any term, the Head must inform the governing body and the LEA.

Grant-maintained and grant-maintained special schools

Similar procedures apply to grant-maintained and grant-maintained special schools under their articles of government, except that notice should be given to the discipline committee of the governing body.

Permanent Exclusions

County, controlled and maintained special schools

The decision to exclude can only be taken by the Head and must be notified to the parents in the same way as for fixed-period exclusions, except that in the case of permanent exclusion, the Head should advise parents of their right of access to the school's curricular records and the other records held on the pupil. Heads are encouraged to respond within 15 days of the request. Heads must notify the LEA and the governing body of all permanent exclusions.

The LEA is under a duty (after consulting with the governing body) to consider whether the permanent exclusion should stand.

Aided and special agreement schools

The same procedures apply, except that the LEA does not have the power to direct reinstatement. The governing body has the duty to decide whether a child should be reinstated.

Grant-maintained and grant-maintained special schools

The key difference is that the schools' instruments and articles of government are set out in the procedures and that the LEA has no role in exclusion procedures. In the case of each type of school, the parent must be informed of their right to appeal to an independent appeals committee.

IMPLICATIONS OF THE SCHOOL STANDARDS AND FRAMEWORK ACT 1998

The **School Standards and Framework Act 1998** repeals all of parts 2 and 3 of the **Education Act 1996**. The procedure for dealing with exclusions will be standardised. The Act sets out the role of the Head and the governing body.

Where the exclusion is a permanent one or one that causes the pupil either to be excluded for more than five school days in a term or lose an opportunity to take a public examination, the Head must inform the governing body and the LEA. The governing body must then:

- consider the circumstances in which the pupil was excluded
- consider any representations about the exclusion made by the parent or (if the pupil is 18 or over) the pupil and by the LEA
- allow the parent (or the pupil if applicable) and an officer of the LEA to attend the hearing and make oral representations
- consider any oral representations.

The governing body has the power to direct the Head to reinstate the pupil. If they decide not to reinstate the pupil, they should inform the parent, the Head and the LEA of their decision and if the pupil is permanently excluded, the parent should be informed of:

- the reasons for the decision

- the right to appeal against the decision

- the person to whom any notice of appeal should be given.

The parent should also be told that any notice of appeal must contain the grounds of appeal, and the last date on which an appeal may be made.

The LEA shall then make arrangements for the parent to appeal against a decision of the governing body not to reinstate a pupil who has been permanently excluded.

Schedule 18 to the **School Standards and Framework Act 1998** sets out how an appeal panel should be constituted. Previously, this was slightly different for county and controlled schools and voluntary-aided and grant-maintained schools. The procedure will be standardised for all schools when these provisions come into force. The new provisions specify that an appeal panel should consist of:

- three or five members appointed by the authority. At least one should be selected from persons who are eligible to be lay members (namely people without personal experience in the management of any school or the provision of education in any school)

- at least one from people who have experience in education or are acquainted with educational conditions in the area of the authority or are parents of registered pupils at a school.

The general principles of natural justice apply and therefore members of the authority, the governing body or people connected to the school authority or pupil are not eligible to sit on the committee.

The LEA has to take reasonable steps to find out what times would be convenient for all those who have the right to attend the hearing.

There are rights for representation at the hearing set out in s.10 of Schedule 18.

1. The appeal panel shall give the relevant person (namely the parent unless the pupil has reached the age of 18) an opportunity of appearing and making oral representations and shall allow him or her to be represented or be accompanied by a friend.

2. The panel shall also allow:

   (a) the Head to make written representations and to appear and make oral representations

   (b) the LEA and the governing body to make written representations

(c) an officer of the authority nominated by the authority and a Governor nominated by the governing body, to appear and make oral representations

(d) the governing body to be represented.

The appeal panel, having concluded that the pupil was guilty of the conduct which the Head relied on as grounds for permanent exclusion, will be required to have regard both to the interests of the excluded pupil and the interests of the other pupils in the school and the school staff and have regard to the discipline measures publicised by the Head in coming to their conclusion.

The decision of an appeal committee and the grounds on which it is made should be communicated by the committee in writing to:

– the relevant person

– the LEA

– the governing body

– the Head.

The letter should be sent by the end of the second school day after the conclusion of the hearing of the appeal. The LEA is not able to reinstate permanently excluded pupils.

Indemnity

Paragraph 5 of schedule 18 of the new **School Standards and Framework Act** provides as follows:

Any local education authority required to make arrangements under Section 67(1) shall indemnify the members of any appeal panel required to be constituted for the purposes of those arrangements against any reasonable legal costs and expenses reasonably incurred by those members in connection with any decision or action taken by them in good faith in pursuance of their functions as members of that panel.

INVESTIGATION OF THE OFFENCE

In *Secretary of State for Education and Science v Tameside Metropolitan Borough Council* [1977] AC 1014, Lord Diplock said

The obligation of the decision maker is to ask the right question and to take reasonable steps to acquaint himself with the relevant information to enable him to answer that question correctly.

In *R v London Borough of Camden and the Governors of Hampstead School, ex parte H* [1996] ELR 360, Lord Justice Kennedy said

Having decided what factual issue or issues they had to resolve and what inquiries they could reasonably make in order to resolve them the Governors and the LEA had to make sure that the inquiries proposed were reasonably thorough.

A recent case looks at how a school went about ascertaining the relevant information. In *R v Roman Catholic Schools ex parte S* [1998] ELR 304, the basic facts were that a serious assault was inflicted on a pupil who was set upon by a number of other pupils in school. There were witnesses, who claimed to have identified two of the pupils. One staff witness, a lunchtime supervisor, made her identification from photographs in the school office. One pupil was excluded and the matter was considered by the governing body who confirmed the exclusion. The pupil appealed to the appeal committee.

The appeal committee relied on the staff member's identification but failed to look at the photographs themselves because they were with the police. The committee did not want to adjourn the hearing (which had already been adjourned twice) because they did not want there to be any further delay in the matter. The committee upheld the child's exclusion. This case needs to be read in its entirety to obtain a full flavour of the issues. The judge confirmed that in cases of this nature, there could be no objection in principle to reliance on hearsay evidence. But he was critical of the committee's failure to probe fully into the circumstances in which the identification of the child had been made. He identified three principles of importance, as follows.

1. Those conducting an inquiry must decide what critical issues of fact they should resolve and what inquiries could reasonably be made to resolve those issues.

2. They must give careful and even-handed consideration to all the available evidence in relation to those issues.

3. Those conducting an enquiry do not need, on every occasion, to carry out searching inquiries involving the calling of bodies of oral evidence.

He said that it would normally be necessary to have oral evidence from the identifying witness to probe the circumstances in which the identification was made. It was incumbent upon those conducting the inquiry to examine carefully the circumstances in which the identification was made and consider the safeguards necessary to avoid the dangers of visual identification were in place. The safeguards included examining:

– the initial description given by the witness of the culprit before the identification took place

– the account of the process of identification (for example how many photographs were shown and what was said)

– the steps taken to avoid any identification being tainted by suggestion.

Any Punishment Should be Appropriate to the Offence

It is a common argument that when decisions to exclude are challenged, there has been not enough regard to less serious penalties.

In *A v Staffordshire County Council* [1996] (The Times, 18 October 1996), the pupil complained that a decision to exclude him permanently from school was disproportionate to the offence of being involved in deflating a teacher's tyres on April Fool's Day. The judge held that the Head and the appeal committee were entitled to have regard to the pupil's poor disciplinary record and the fact that his continued presence at the school would make it more difficult for the school to deliver satisfactory education to the rest of the children. The court upheld the decision of the appeal committee.

R v Solihull Borough Council, ex parte W [1997] 4 ELR 489 QBD, concerned an alleged incident involving the applicant brandishing a knife. As a result, the applicant was excluded permanently from school. The applicant made an application for judicial review challenging the decision of the council's appeal committee to reject his appeal against permanent exclusion. It was held that the decision by the appeal committee was not irrational. Where there was, as in this case, behaviour which was potentially as dangerous as the wielding of an open knife, it was open to the appropriate authorities to conclude that exclusion was the right response.

IMPORTANCE OF COMPLYING WITH THE DfEE CIRCULAR

R v Governing Body of The Rectory School and the London Borough of Richmond ex parte WK (A Minor) [1997] 4 ELR 484 QBD concerned an application for leave to move for judicial review of a decision to exclude a child for 15 days and a later decision to uphold the Head's decision to exclude the child permanently. Basically, the complaint was of procedural unfairness. As the fixed-term exclusion was for the maximum aggregate period per term permitted by law, the only further exclusion possible when a subsequent incident occurred was permanent exclusion. The application was based on the failure to provide the child's mother with an opportunity to make representations in respect of the fixed-term exclusion. The judge held that, having regard to the legislation and Circular 10/94, there was a duty on the LEA or the Governors of a school to arrange a meeting for the purposes of hearing the parent's representations. He granted leave to apply for judicial review.

This case illustrates the fact that although the Circular is not mandatory, being only guidance where the question of reasonableness arises, whether the guidance has been followed is relevant in determining the outcome of the case.

R v Northamptonshire County Council, ex parte W [1998] 3 ELR 291 QBD, is also important for the judge's comments regarding the guidance in Circular 10/94. Section 68 of the **School Standards and Framework Act 1998** introduces a specific statutory requirement for Heads, Governors, LEAs and appeal committees to have regard to the guidance (which in any event is being revised) when making an exclusion decision. Even without this new requirement, the Circular's guidance should be taken into account by the appeal committee.

> There is a submission...that the committee were not obliged as a matter of
> law to have regard to the Circular. I do not think that can be right.

Reasons Why the Exclusion was Justified

The appeal committee must give its reasons why the extreme measure of exclusion was justified. In one case, D was aged 7. He suffered from dyspraxia. D was excluded permanently from school for misbehaviour. The exclusion was upheld by the governing body and by the LEA. The appeal committee rejected the appeal.

The letter to the parents stated that D had been found to have been responsible for the actions which resulted in his exclusion and that the Committee had been satisfied that permanent exclusion was "in the circumstances, a reasonable course of action for the school". Schedule 16, para 14 to the **Education Act 1996** stated that "The decision of an appeal committee and the grounds on which it is made shall be communicated by the committee in writing to the [parents], the local education authority and the governing body".

D sought judicial review of the committee's decision. He contended that the letter to his parents did not comply with the statutory requirement to give reasons and that the defect could not be cured by the affidavit of the chairwoman of the appeal committee, Mrs Gwynne, which explained the factors which had weighed with the committee. The court agreed that the letter had to explain to the parents why D was being excluded. In this case it felt that affidavit by the chairwoman of the appeals committee cured the defect.

CONCLUSION

The following points emerge:

- the governing body must have regard to DfEE Circular 10/94
- procedures must be followed and all those who have rights of representation must be notified of their rights and heard
- the governing body must bear in mind the principles of natural justice and proportionality
- the governing body must ensure that they make sufficient investigations into the nature of the incident.

INDEX